**WITHDRAWN**

# THE WIZARD OF OZ

*Shaping an Imaginary World*

# TWAYNE'S MASTERWORK STUDIES

*Robert Lecker, General Editor*

# THE WIZARD OF OZ

## *Shaping an Imaginary World*

Suzanne Rahn

TWAYNE PUBLISHERS

*New York*

Twayne's Masterwork Studies No. 167

*The Wizard of Oz: Shaping an Imaginary World*
Suzanne Rahn

Twayne Publishers

1633 Broadway
New York, NY 10019

**Library of Congress Cataloging-in-Publication Data**
Rahn, Suzanne.
    The Wizard of Oz : shaping an imaginary world / Suzanne Rahn.
      p.   cm.—(Twayne's masterwork studies ; no. 167)
    Includes bibliographical references (p.   ) and index.
    ISBN 0-8057-8623-6 (alk. paper)
    1. Baum, L. Frank (Lyman Frank), 1856–1919. Wizard of Oz.
    2. Fantastic fiction, American—History and criticism.   3. Oz
(Imaginary place)  I. Title.  II. Series.
PS3503.A923W637   1998
813'.4—dc21                             98-6751
                                           CIP

10 9 8 7 6 5 4 3 2

Printed in the United States of America

*This one is for Sherry.*

L. Frank Baum, circa 1915.
*Used by permission of the* Baum Bugle.

# Contents

# Acknowledgments

Albert Wendland's *Science, Myth, and the Fictional Creation of Alien Worlds* (Ann Arbor: UMI Research Press, 1985), with its system of classification for alien worlds, prompted my thinking about different ways of seeing the "landscape" of Oz. Discussions with my students, whose enjoyment of *The Wizard* was an inspiration in itself, helped to generate many of the ideas in the "Approaches to Teaching" appendix. I would also like to thank William Stillman, editor of the *Baum Bugle,* for his helpful responses to my queries and his permission to use illustrations from the *Bugle* and *The Oz Toy Book.* The loving encouragement and support of my husband, John, and my mother, Mary Henry, have been, as always, indispensable. The encouragement of my friend Sherry Jones has also been of inestimable value to me over a period of many years; to her I dedicate this book.

# Note on the References

The edition I have used is *The Wizard of Oz* by L. Frank Baum, edited by Michael Patrick Hearn, in the Critical Heritage Series (New York: Schocken Books, 1983).

# Chronology: L. Frank Baum's Life and Works

| | |
|---|---|
| 1856 | Lyman Frank Baum born on 15 May in Chittenango, New York, the seventh of nine children, to Cynthia Stanton Baum and Benjamin Ward Baum, a prosperous oilman and banker. |
| 1861 | The Baum family moves to "Rose Lawn," a country estate near Syracuse, New York. Frank, a shy child with a heart defect, is schooled at home and spends much of his time alone with imaginary playmates or with his flock of bantam chickens. |
| 1868–1870 | Is sent to Peekskill Military Academy and hates it; after a severe illness, he is finally allowed to stay home. |
| 1871–1874 | Edits an amateur newspaper, *The Rose Lawn Home Journal*, with his brother Harry. In 1874, joins a theater company under the name of George Brooks. |
| 1877 | Gets his first professional newspaper job, with *The New Era* in Bradford, Pennsylvania. |
| 1878 | Decides to be an actor and joins the Union Square Theatre company in New York City. |
| 1882 | Organizes an acting company, financed by his father, and goes on tour, playing the lead in his own *The Maid of Arran*, a sentimental melodrama. Despite good reviews and a two-year run, the play fails to make a profit. Also marries Maud Gage, over the strong opposition of her mother. |
| 1883 | His first child, Frank Joslyn, is born. Baum proves a gentle and loving father who enjoys playing with and telling stories to his children. |
| 1884 | Loses a chain of small theaters deeded to him by his father. |
| 1885 | Becomes the principal salesman for Baum's Castorine, an axle grease made from crude oil. |
| 1886 | Publishes his first book, *The Book of the Hamburgs*, a treatise on breeding and raising Hamburg chickens. A second son, Robert, is born. |

| | |
|---|---|
| 1887 | Deaths of Benjamin Baum and his oldest son. The family fortune declines, and Baum's Castorine goes out of business. Frank and Maud join Maud's brother in Aberdeen, a small prairie town in Dakota Territory. Edward Bellamy publishes his influential utopia, *Looking Backward.* |
| 1887–1889 | Baum opens a general store called "Baum's Bazaar" with his remaining capital. But Aberdeen is sinking into depression; Baum extends too much credit, and the Bazaar goes under, two weeks after the birth of a third son, Harry. |
| 1890–1891 | Takes over a weekly newspaper, *The Aberdeen Saturday Pioneer.* Although his satirical column "Our Landlady" is popular, circulation gradually shrinks and the paper fails. Three days later, a fourth son, Kenneth, is born. The family moves to Chicago, where Baum works first for the *Evening Post,* then for a department store. In England, in 1891, William Morris publishes his socialist utopia, *News from Nowhere.* |
| 1892 | Baum becomes a traveling salesman selling china and glassware for Pitkin and Brooks. |
| 1893 | A severe two-year depression grips the nation's economy, but Chicago's Columbian Exposition is a huge success. |
| 1896 | Baum marches in torchlight parades for Democratic presidential candidate William Jennings Bryan after hearing his "Cross of Gold" speech at the National Convention in Chicago. Bryan loses to William McKinley. |
| 1897 | Publishes his first children's book, *Mother Goose in Prose,* a collection of stories based on Mother Goose rhymes and illustrated by Maxfield Parrish. Also publishes a volume of poetry, *By the Candelabra's Glare,* and founds *The Show Window,* "a journal of practical, up-to-date window trimming." Becomes founder and first president of the National Association of Window Trimmers of America. |
| 1898 | The Spanish-American War. On 7 May, news of Admiral Dewey's victory in Manila reaches Chicago; according to family tradition, the Land of Oz is named on this day. |
| 1899 | Publishes *Father Goose,* a book of comic verse illustrated by W. W. Denslow. With the profits from this success, buys a summer cottage in the Michigan resort town of Macatawa, calling it "The Sign of the Goose." |
| 1900 | Publishes *The Wonderful Wizard of Oz,* with illustrations by Denslow. Also produces three other children's books: *The Army Alphabet, The Navy Alphabet,* and a collection of fairy tales called *A New Wonderland.* Publishes *The Art of Decorating,* a handbook on decorating store windows and interiors. |

# Chronology

1901      Publishes *The Master Key: An Electrical Fairy Tale*—a science fiction story for boys—and *Dot and Tot of Merryland*, a fantasy and his last collaboration with Denslow.

1902      The *Wizard of Oz* is adapted into a stage musical, which opens in Chicago and is a smash success there and on Broadway. Publishes *The Life and Adventures of Santa Claus*, a serious fantasy "explaining" the existence of Santa Claus. Hands over *The Show Window* to a new editor, intending to devote his energy to children's books.

1903      Publishes *The Enchanted Island of Yew*, an unsuccessful fantasy.

1904      Yields to children's demands for "more about Oz" and publishes *The Marvelous Land of Oz* (later known as *The Land of Oz*), the only Oz book in which Dorothy does not appear. Important new characters include Jack Pumpkinhead, the Sawhorse, the Woggle-Bug, and Princess Ozma, the new ruler of Oz. The illustrator, John R. Neill, will continue to illustrate Oz books by Baum and others until his death in 1943. Baum creates a syndicated weekly newspaper comic page, *Queer Visitors from the Marvelous Land of Oz,* in which the Scarecrow, the Tin Woodman, Jack Pumpkinhead, the Sawhorse, and the Woggle-Bug visit the United States; this runs through February 1905. Begins spending winters at the Hotel del Coronado in southern California.

1905      Publishes *The Woggle-Bug Book,* a picture book about the Woggle-Bug's American adventures, as advance publicity for a new stage production, *The Woggle-Bug*—an expensive failure. Also publishes *Animal Fairy Tales* and *Queen Zixi of Ix*, considered by many critics one of his finest children's books. As "Schuyler Staunton," publishes his first novel for adults, a romantic adventure story called *The Fate of a Crown.*

1906      Publishes *John Dough and the Cherub*, a farcical fantasy, and the first of the highly successful "Aunt Jane's Nieces" series (under the name "Edith Van Dyne"). Sails with Maud to Europe for a six-month vacation trip through Egypt, Greece, Italy, Switzerland, and France.

1907      Publishes *Ozma of Oz*, the third Oz book, reintroducing Dorothy and including several popular new characters— Billina the talking hen, Tik-Tok the mechanical man, the Hungry Tiger, and the villainous Nome King.

1908      Publishes the fourth Oz book, *Dorothy and the Wizard of Oz,* in which the Wizard returns to Oz and settles there. Also publishes *American Fairy Tales*—tales of "modern fairies" with an American setting; an anonymous adult novel, *The Last*

*Egyptian;* and the first of a series for boys, *The Boy Fortune Hunters* (as "Floyd Akers"). Invests—and loses—large sums of money in a series of productions based on his stories, which he calls "Fairylogues and Radio Plays."

1909    Publishes *The Road to Oz,* the fifth Oz book, considered one of his poorest. New characters include Button-Bright, an American boy; Polychrome, the daughter of the Rainbow; and the Shaggy Man.

1910    Publishes *The Emerald City of Oz,* the sixth Oz book, which he intends to be the last. Dorothy's Aunt Em and Uncle Henry come to live with her in Oz, and the story ends with Oz cut off forever from the outside world. The Baums themselves move to California, where they build a house in Hollywood called "Ozcot."

1911    Publishes *The Sea Fairies,* featuring a little California girl named Trot and her friend Cap'n Bill. Following the financial disaster of the "Fairylogues and Radio Plays," Baum is forced to declare bankruptcy. Letters from children demand a return to Oz.

1912    Publishes *Sky Island,* another story about Trot and Cap'n Bill.

1913    Pressured by the wishes of countless children as well as economic necessity, publishes a seventh Oz book, *The Patchwork Girl of Oz.* Finally resigned to being "Royal Historian of Oz," Baum explains that he has succeeded in reestablishing contact with Oz by wireless telegraph. Meanwhile, his latest stage venture, *The Tik-Tok Man of Oz,* opens in Los Angeles for a successful run.

1914    Publishes *Tik-Tok of Oz,* the eighth Oz book. Also forms the Oz Film Manufacturing Company to produce movies based on his own stories. Five films are completed before the company fails.

1915    Publishes *The Scarecrow of Oz,* the ninth Oz book.

1916    Publishes *Rinkitink in Oz,* the 10th Oz book.

1917    Publishes *The Lost Princess of Oz,* the 11th Oz book.

1918    Publishes *The Tin Woodman of Oz,* the 12th Oz book. Is confined to bed by heart problems and a gallbladder operation but continues writing.

1919    Publishes *The Magic of Oz,* the 13th Oz book. On 5 May, at the age of 62, suffers a stroke and dies the next day, with Maud at his bedside.

1920    *Glinda of Oz,* the 14th Oz book, is published posthumously, and Baum's publisher hires Ruth Plumly Thompson to continue the series. The new Royal Historian will write 19 Oz books before her retirement in 1939.

# LITERARY AND
# HISTORICAL
# CONTEXT

# 1

# The Historical Context

In 1882 Frank Baum—he disliked his first name, Lyman, and never used it—proposed to Maud Gage. Maud was only 20, a student at Cornell University, and her mother, the well-known suffragist Matilda Joslyn Gage, vehemently opposed the marriage. The 25-year-old Baum was a good-looking young man, dark-haired with gentle gray eyes and over six feet tall, but he seemed a poor choice for her youngest and best-loved child.

Owing to a heart defect, Baum's childhood had been a sheltered one; his wealthy and indulgent father had given him what he wanted, from a flock of bantam chickens to a printing press. His formal schooling consisted of two unhappy years at a military academy in his early teens. He had tried his hand first at newspaper reporting, then at acting. He had written a melodrama and, financed by his father, organized a theater company to produce it, with himself in the leading role. *The Maid of Arran* had received good reviews; Baum's father had even invested in a chain of small theaters, which he intended to hand over to his son. Yet the theater was a risky profession, and actors notoriously poor husbands. *The Maid of Arran* ran for two years but never turned a substantial profit. And Baum was clearly less interested in managing the theater chain than in writing new plays.

Frank waited in the front parlor while Maud argued with her mother. "I won't have my daughter be a darned fool and marry an actor," snapped Mrs. Gage.[1] But Maud was as strong-willed as her mother. She won the argument and married Frank that November.

Though the marriage itself was happy, the years that followed saw the realization of Mrs. Gage's worst fears, as Baum failed in one business venture after another. The theater chain, entrusted to a book-keeper, was so mismanaged that it had to be sold to pay creditors. Baum became a salesman for Baum's Castorine, an axle grease manu-factured by his older brother, but after his father and brother both died in 1887, the business fell apart. Maud and Frank went west to Aberdeen, a small prairie town in Dakota Territory, and invested their remaining capital in a variety store that they called Baum's Bazaar; before two years were up, it failed, and the bank foreclosed. With less than a hundred dollars left, Baum bought a weekly newspaper, *The Aberdeen Saturday Pioneer*—in a town that already had two weeklies and a daily. The paper went under; as Baum wryly put it, "The sheriff wanted the paper more than I did—so I let him have it" (Baum and MacFall, 74).

By now Frank and Maud had four children: Frank Joslyn, Robert, Harry, and Kenneth. In 1891 they moved to Chicago, strug-gling to survive on Baum's inadequate salaries—first as a reporter, then as a buyer for a department store, then as a traveling salesman selling china and glassware, while Maud gave embroidery lessons. He was a good salesman, and slowly the family finances began to improve.

All his life, however, Frank Baum would remain prone to finan-cial disaster. Even years later, after achieving success and popularity as a writer, he would sink large sums of money into spectacular ventures that ended—sometimes literally—in bankruptcy. Yet in some ways the pattern of his life was merely typical of the age in which he lived.

The post–Civil War decades in America were a time of unprece-dented economic growth. Business interests became dominant in American society, as new industries—oil, steel, meatpacking, railroads, department stores—were structured into mammoth corporations. Industrial capitalists like Andrew Carnegie, John D. Rockefeller, Cornelius Vanderbilt, and J. P. Morgan became the most powerful men in the country. Frank Baum's father, Benjamin, was a small part of this picture; son of a country minister, he became one of the nation's first oil producers, a wealthy man with his own country estate. Yet the period was also one of increasing division between rich and poor, of rampant corruption in business and government, of devastating panics and depressions, of fortunes lost as well as made. With the deaths of Benjamin and his oldest son, the Baum family's prosperity melted away like the Wicked Witch of the West, and the country estate where Frank had spent his happy childhood was sold.

Baum's many and varied ventures, the recurrent rise and fall of his personal fortunes, were not unusual in this age of speculation. Mark Twain, America's most successful author, invested enormous sums to develop a typesetting machine and establish his own publishing firm, and was driven into bankruptcy in 1893 when both ventures failed.

Thousands sought their fortunes in the West, and many, like Frank and Maud, arrived at precisely the wrong time. After the good farming years of the early 1880s came a decade of frost and drought; crops failed in all but two years between 1886 and 1895. Countless settlers abandoned their homesteads—including Almanzo and Laura Ingalls Wilder, who left the Dakota Territory for Missouri in 1894. Others returned East, their covered wagons painted with the sardonic legend:

> In God We Trusted
> In Kansas We Busted.

Baum was a poor businessman who extended too much credit to his customers, but as Aberdeen sank deep into depression in the late 1880s, few new enterprises could have made a profit there.

The move to Chicago, on the other hand, could not have been a better choice. Mushrooming from frontier outpost to industrial metropolis in two generations, twice destroyed by fire and twice reborn bigger, richer, and more vigorous than before, this phenomenal city was the nerve center of America's shift westward. In 1893, with all of America in the grip of a two-year depression, Chicago found the resources to host the World's Columbian Exposition—the largest world's fair in history. Here Baum finally learned how to channel his creative energies into commercial success. Baum's Bazaar had shown him the importance of effective window displays, while his theatrical background had taught him a good deal about scenery, lighting, and special effects that could be applied to the new craft of window decoration. In 1897 he persuaded a local publisher to finance a trade journal for window dressers, *The Show Window,* with himself as editor. He went on to found the first National Association of Window Trimmers and wrote a definitive handbook on the subject, *The Art of Decorating.* These enterprises made it possible for him to quit his job as traveling salesman and give more time to his creative writing.

Even more important for Baum's future as a writer, Chicago was in the midst of a cultural renaissance. The exposition inspired a generation of architects and city planners. Louis Sullivan and Frank Lloyd Wright were creating an architectural aesthetic for the twentieth century. Writers like Frank Norris, Hamlin Garland, and Harriet Monroe were making Chicago a center of literary experimentation. For the first time, Baum found himself in a community of writers, artists, and publishers. His early children's books would have pictures by Maxfield Parrish and W. W. Denslow, two of the finest illustrators in the country. Without the stimulus and the opportunities of Chicago, Baum would always have been a storyteller, but might never have become an author.

He had always loved telling his own stories to children—not only to his four sons but also to the children who clustered around him on the wooden sidewalks of Aberdeen or in the living room in Chicago. And at the turn of the century, children's literature was flourishing in America; there was a ready market for what he wanted most to write.

Fantasy, however, had developed much more slowly in America than in Britain. In Britain, the Golden Age of children's literature that began with *Alice's Adventures in Wonderland* in 1865 was associated (though not exclusively) with authors of fantasy, such as Lewis Carroll, George MacDonald, Rudyard Kipling, and E. Nesbit. In America, authors of the here and now, like Louisa May Alcott and Mark Twain, had dominated the field. American fantasy had consisted mainly of reworked European material—Hawthorne's retellings of Greek myths in *A Wonder-Book,* for example, or Washington Irving's recasting of German legend in "Rip Van Winkle," or Charles Carryl's blatant imitation of the "Alice" books in *Davy and the Goblin.* Even these tended to be short stories—fairy tales rather than full-length fantasies. It was as though American authors could not sustain a flight of fantasy—even on borrowed wings.[2]

Baum's first children's book, *Mother Goose in Prose* (1897), fit the established pattern, consisting of short tales that expanded on traditional British rhymes. His second, *Father Goose* (1899), was merely a book of mildly comic verse. But in 1900 came *The Wonderful Wizard of Oz*—not only the first successful full-length fantasy by an American author, but the first to create a distinctly American imaginary world.

# 2

# The Importance of *The Wizard of Oz*

Even if children today knew nothing of *The Wizard of Oz,* its place in the history of children's literature would be secure. After Oz, the stream of American fantasy for children flowed freely and fully, not least from Baum himself; *The Wizard* was only his first of 14 Oz books and numerous other fantasies. A lifelong lover of fairy tales who had written a scholarly introduction on Mother Goose for *Mother Goose in Prose,* Baum was quite aware that he was attempting something new. He claims in the introduction to *The Wizard* that "the old-time fairy tale, having served for generations, may now be classed as 'historical' in the children's library; for the time has come for a series of newer 'wonder tales' in which the stereotyped genie, dwarf and fairy are eliminated, together with all the horrible and bloodcurdling incident devised by their authors to point a fearsome moral to each tale." *The Wizard* was to be "a modernized fairy tale, in which the wonderment and joy are retained and the heart-aches and nightmares are left out."[1]

But Baum's pioneering achievement lay not so much in the absence of morals and nightmares as in his discovery of how to infuse American rather than European elements into the ancient form of the fairy tale. *The Wizard* follows the traditional pattern of the magical quest story, in which a hero and his companions (usually all male) go in search of something virtually unobtainable yet infinitely desirable—the Water of Life, the Golden Bird, the dragon's treasure hoard—and at last, after a long and hazardous journey, find what they are seeking. *The Wizard,* however, begins not in some kingdom "once upon a time," but in Kansas. Its protagonist is a little American girl, her first companion in her quest a typical American scarecrow, and the mighty Wizard a con man from Omaha. The goal of her quest is simply to return home to Kansas. The Land of Oz itself has a more subtle yet unmistakably American flavor—as I show later, in my analysis of Baum's imaginary world.

Apart from its historical significance, *The Wizard* remains one of the best-known and best-loved children's books ever written. It has been a favorite ever since it was published, nearly a hundred years ago—in fact, it is one of the top-selling titles of the century. Despite its strongly American character, it has proved its universality by having been translated into nearly every major language, including Chinese, Japanese, Portuguese, Romanian, Polish, Swedish, Turkish, Russian, Czech, Hungarian, Hebrew, and Bengali. Many of its readers have testified in later life how much the Oz books meant to them as children.

Yet for most children, *The Wizard of Oz* is the name of a movie, not a book. It is the MGM film version of 1939 that has made the story a cultural icon, whose scenes, symbols, and characters convey an instantly recognizable complex of meanings for virtually every American with a television set. Only moderately successful on its first release—the Oscars that year went overwhelmingly to *Gone with the Wind*—the movie made its television premiere in 1956. By the 1970s, watching *The Wizard* had become an annual ritual for thousands of families. The movie has been seen by as many as 50 million viewers in a single showing and at least a billion times altogether, more times than any other movie in history.[2]

As a result, Baum's story has permeated American culture. A reference to the Wizard of Oz, to the Tin Woodman, to the Yellow Brick Road, to Munchkins—even to Toto—is understood by millions who have never read the book or heard of L. Frank Baum. Aided by its strong visual imagery and clear symbolic structure, the story has become a kind of myth and, like a myth, can be alluded to, translated, and transformed again and again in myriad ways.

References to *The Wizard* are everywhere—in cartoons, advertisements, comic strips, popular songs, television shows, and science fiction stories. Scarcely a political crisis or campaign occurs without some indignant mention of the humbug Wizard behind the curtain. The first attempt by American astronomers to make radio contact with intelligent beings from other solar systems was named by its director, Frank D. Drake, "Project Ozma." Not surprisingly, many references are specific to the film version; the Ruby Slippers, for example, are referred to more often than the Silver Shoes of the original story. Certain lines have acquired their own fame: "Somewhere, over the rainbow," "Toto, I've a feeling we're not in Kansas anymore," "Follow the Yellow Brick Road,"and "I'm melting!"[3]

The universal familiarity of *The Wizard* makes it ideal for commercial purposes. Abridged, pop-up, and coloring book versions of the story have appeared in great numbers, as well as *Wizard of Oz* games, puzzles, dolls, puppets, greeting cards, mugs, T-shirts, music boxes, Christmas tree ornaments, bath mats, woolen gloves, and stained-glass window panels. Places and institutions claim association with Oz, in an attempt to shine in its reflected glow. Chittenango, New York, Baum's birthplace, has had a yellow brick sidewalk installed and stages an annual parade to commemorate his birthday. The Visitor Bureau of Coronado, California, where Baum spent several winters, heads an advertisement "Across the bridge and over the rainbow... Coronado." A Kansas postcard shows Dorothy and her companions, with the caption "Kansas—There is no place like home." Chicago has an Oz Park. Seattle calls itself the Emerald City. A recent ad boosting the Smithsonian Institution featured a life-size glittering photograph of the Ruby Slippers, now in its possession, with the thrice-repeated caption "There's no place like the Smithsonian." In 1970 a pair of ruby slippers used in the film was auctioned for $15,000.[4]

Like many myths and folktales, *The Wizard* has been translated into other art forms, beginning with the stage musical of 1902.

Numerous films and plays have been based on or inspired by the story, including the all-black musical *The Wiz* (1975), the science fiction film *Zardoz* (1974), and more than one extravaganza on ice. And writers have drawn upon both Baum's original and the MGM film. Ray Bradbury's "The Exiles" (1951), Philip José Farmer's *A Barnstormer in Oz* (1982), Geoff Ryman's *Was* (1992), Salman Rushdie's "At the Auction of the Ruby Slippers" (1992), and Gregory Maguire's *Wicked: The Life and Times of the Wicked Witch of the West* (1995) have all found in Baum's fantasy a way of framing ideas about childhood, evil, utopia, the power of imagination, the loss of innocence, and the desire for home.

This mythic quality has given *The Wizard of Oz* a special place in children's literature. For this reason, as well as for its own sake, it is worthy of close and appreciative critical attention.

# 3

# The Critical Reception

Most people wouldn't hesitate to call *The Wizard of Oz* a classic of American children's literature. Yet if a children's classic can be defined as a book that is admired by critics and loved by children, then *The Wizard* belongs in a peculiar category of its own. Enthusiastically received by the first reviewers, the Oz books fell into such disfavor with children's librarians 30 years later that they were systematically purged from library collections. For decades, standard references on children's literature either disparaged the series or omitted it completely. Only parents who had loved the books as children and wanted to share them—and children who continued to enjoy them—kept the books in print. Then, in the 1970s, the pendulum swung again. The last 20 years have seen a renewed acceptance and appreciation of the Oz books, accompanied by critical analyses from the full gamut of perspectives—political, economic, spiritual, feminist, and psychological. The MGM film version of *The Wizard,* too, has received careful study and increasing respect. Yet reservations are still expressed; while no one today would deny the cultural importance of *The Wizard,* its quality as literature remains somewhat in doubt.

*The Wonderful Wizard of Oz*—its original title—was the best-selling children's book of 1900. A Baum family story relates that

Frank, who had no idea how well the book was doing, went to his publisher for an advance of $100 to buy Christmas presents for his children. He took the check home without looking at it and gave it to Maud, who handled all the household finances. Maud was ironing. When she saw that the check was for $3,432.64, she forgot the hot iron and burned a hole in Frank's only other shirt (Carpenter and Shirley, 59).

The reviews, too, were better than Frank could have expected. Many compared *The Wizard* to *Alice in Wonderland,* not simply because both were stories of a young girl exploring an imaginary world, but in terms of quality. Much of the praise was for W. W. Denslow's illustrations and striking color design. As Michael Patrick Hearn points out in *The Annotated Wizard of Oz,* few contemporary children's books made such lavish and innovative use of color.[1] In addition to 24 color plates, Denslow had done numerous smaller text illustrations in which black and white were combined with a single color that matched the changing color scheme indicated in the story. Thus, the opening chapters, with their drab Kansas setting, were highlighted in dull sepia, which changed in the land of the blue-loving Munchkins to a pleasant bluish green—then to poppy red as the travelers entered the Deadly Poppy Field—then to emerald green as they approached the Emerald City—and so on throughout the book.

But reviewers also predicted that Baum's story would have great appeal for children. "Little folk will go wild over it," declared the *Bookseller and Latest Literature,* and the *New York Times* agreed that "it will indeed be strange if there be a normal child who will not enjoy the story" (Hearn 1973, 34, 36). The *Times* reviewer also commented on "the bright and joyous atmosphere" of *The Wizard,* on "the living and breathing quality" of characters like the Scarecrow and the Tin Woodman, and on Baum's ability to stretch the minds of young readers: "The story has humor and here and there stray bits of philosophy that will be a moving power on the child mind and will furnish fields of study and investigation for the future students and professors of psychology" (35). A Philadelphia newspaper review quoted in *Book News* similarly realized that *The Wizard* might appeal to adults as well as children: "It is not lacking in philosophy and satire which will furnish amusement to the adult and cause the juvenile to think some new and healthy thoughts" (34).

The later Oz books, however, did not receive much notice from the major periodicals, perhaps because Baum's publishers, Reilly and Britton (later Reilly and Lee), did not bother to do much advertising.[2] They knew that the latest Oz book would always be a best-seller. Baum himself had never intended a sequel to *The Wizard*. He was eager to move on to other experiments in fantasy. But the success of the stage musical version of *The Wizard of Oz* in 1902 motivated him to write another Oz book that could also be adapted for the stage; the theater, after all, was his first love, whose siren call he was never able to resist. Besides, children were begging for "more about Oz." In 1904, he published *The Land of Oz,* a sequel explaining how Oz came to be ruled by the fairy princess Ozma; this became, in turn, a new stage musical called *The Woggle-Bug* (1905). Unfortunately, *The Woggle-Bug* was an expensive flop. Financial necessity forced Baum not only to write more Oz books but to turn to hack writing, publishing whole series of books for young people under various pseudonyms.

With the sixth Oz book, *The Emerald City of Oz* (1910), Baum made one last attempt to end the series. Dorothy brings her Aunt Em and Uncle Henry from Kansas (where they are about to lose the heavily mortgaged farm) to live with her and Ozma in the Emerald City, and Ozma decides to cut Oz off forever from the outside world. Once more, however, the "Royal Historian of Oz" discovered that none of his other children's books were as popular—or sold as well—as the Oz books. His forays into the new medium of film had proved even more disastrous financially than *The Woggle-Bug*. In 1913 he announced in *The Patchwork Girl of Oz* that he had reestablished contact with Oz by wireless telegraph. From then until his death six years later, a new Oz book appeared each year, just before Christmas.

Even Baum's death did not bring an end to the series. Reluctant to see their cash cow dry up, Baum's publishers got Maud Baum's permission to hire a new Royal Historian. Ruth Plumly Thompson wrote 19 Oz books before her retirement in 1939—five more than Baum himself. Three more Oz books were written by John R. Neill, who had illustrated all the Oz books except the first; two more by Jack Snow; another by Rachel R. Cosgrove; and two more by Eloise Jarvis McGraw and Lauren McGraw Wagner. One cannot say even today that the series has come to an end, as several additional writers have tried their hand in recent years.

Meanwhile, in 1929, the first scholarly analysis of the Oz books had appeared. Edward Wagenknecht's pamphlet, *Utopia Americana,* is particularly noteworthy as one of the earliest literary analyses—outside of book reviews—of any children's author. After defending fantasy as a genre, Wagenknecht suggested that the Oz books represent "the first distinctive attempt to construct a fairyland out of American materials" and "may even be considered an American utopia."[3] Although he did not develop any of these points in detail, he realized the pivotal part played by the Oz books in the history of American fantasy and raised issues that later critics would also find of great interest: the reflection of American culture in the Oz books and their utopian aspect. And he was the first of many to see in the Oz books a kind of flagship for the realm of the imagination, to stand or fall with Faerie itself.

Only shortly afterward came the first assault on the Oz books. Anne Carroll Moore was, at this time, unquestionably the most influential figure in the field of American children's librarianship. Since 1906, she had been head of the children's department of New York City's library system. She was the first to chair the newly inaugurated Children's Librarians' section of the American Library Association, and her thoughtful reviews of children's books for the *New York Herald Tribune* aimed at creating a higher standard for American children's literature. In the 1930s Moore suddenly removed the entire series of Oz books from the Central Children's Room of the New York Public Library. At a publisher's press reception, the bewildered Ruth Plumly Thompson asked Moore to explain her decision, but Moore refused, then or ever, to make her reasons public (Hearn 1983, xi). All over New York City and across the country, other children's librarians promptly followed her lead.

The Oz books had, in effect, been blacklisted by the American children's literature establishment. And in the 1950s came another wave of condemnation. Ralph Uveling, director of the Detroit library system, announced that he was keeping the Oz books out of the children's departments because there was "nothing uplifting or elevating about the Baum series." The Oz books were of "no value" and presented "a cowardly approach to life" (Hearn 1983, xiii).[4] Florida State Librarian Dorothy Dodd agreed, classifying them with other popular series as "poorly written, untrue to life," and "foolishly sentimental," and recommending that they be removed from Florida library collections (Carpenter and Shirley, 134). A Washington librarian, Elva Van Winkle, ordered *The Wizard* withdrawn because it was "dated and stiff" (quoted by Gallico in Hearn 1983, 183). Two major reference works on children's literature, May Hill Arbuthnot's *Children and Books* (1947) and the 624-page *A Critical History of Children's Literature* (1953) edited by Cornelia Meigs had simply omitted any mention of *The Wizard* or the other Oz books.[5]

To adults who had loved the books as children, the librarians' explanations were as baffling as their silence. But Oz did not lack defenders. The *Detroit Times* countered Uveling's ban by publishing *The Wizard* in serial installments (Carpenter and Shirley, 134). And in 1934, in his essay "The Wizard of Chittenango," the great humorist James Thurber became the first of many distinguished writers to reassess and praise the Oz books. Essays in defense of Oz have been written by the novelists Paul Gallico, Shirley Jackson, and Gore Vidal; the critic Clifton Fadiman; the science writer Martin Gardner; the science fiction writer Ray Bradbury; and the historians Russel B. Nye and C. Warren Hollister.[6]

While the centenary of Baum's birth in 1956 witnessed renewed attacks on the Oz books, it also inspired new scholarly interest in his work. Martin Gardner and Russel B. Nye published the first critical edition of *The Wizard* in 1957, accompanied by analytical and biographical essays.[7] The first full-length biography of Baum, *To Please a Child,* by Frank Joslyn Baum and Russell P. MacFall, came out in 1961. In 1956 at Columbia University, Roland S. Baughman, the head of Special Collections, mounted the first retrospective exhibition of Baum's work—which became, in turn, the debut of the next generation of Oz scholars. As the exhibition catalog explains,

> After the exhibition was installed and the catalogue copy was in the hands of the printer, we were visited by Mr. Justin Schiller, aged 12, who, it developed, is an ardent collector of L. Frank Baum. He brought with him a number of significant items, some of which we had sought for vainly when the exhibition was being prepared, and some which we had not known existed. Mr. Schiller has graciously permitted us to include selected items from his library in this display. (Carpenter and Shirley, 130)

At 13, Justin Schiller—in part as a response to the librarians' attacks on Baum—organized a small group of fellow Oz fans into the International Wizard of Oz Club and began publishing a club journal, which he named *The Baum Bugle*. The IWOC now has several thousand members, organizes annual conventions, and has done much to promote Baum's recognition as an important children's author. *The Baum Bugle* has grown from a mimeographed newsletter to a handsomely produced and illustrated semischolarly journal that is the main source of scholarship on Baum, his work, and the entire Oz series.

All this interest in Baum made it more difficult to pretend that the Oz books did not exist, and the same reference works that had previously ignored them began to include them in revised editions—though never without dispraise. Although Baum was still omitted entirely from the 1964 (third) edition of *Children and Books,* Zena Sutherland's later revisions allowed him two sentences in a section entitled "Books That Stir Controversy." According to the 1991 (eighth) edition, *"The Wizard of Oz* and, to a lesser degree, its sequels have remained favorites of many children despite the fact that many authorities in the field of children's literature feel that the style is flat and dull, and that the inventiveness of the first book was followed by mediocrity and repetition in subsequent volumes."[8] In the 1969 edition of *A Critical History of Children's Literature,* Ruth Hill Viguers similarly explained that "inventive though it was, *The Wizard of Oz* (1900) was told in such lifeless prose that rereading it in adulthood is a disappointment. Because there is no grace in the style, no subtlety in the storytelling to give conviction to the fantastic people and incidents, it lost nothing in translation to the screen."[9] Even in more recent reference works and children's literature textbooks, the same note of disparakement is sounded. Though *The Oxford Companion to Children's Literature* (1984), by Humphrey Carpenter and Mari Prichard, concedes Baum's importance in the history of American children's literature, it also declares that

> Baum's writing cannot be called distinguished. Even *The Wonderful Wizard of Oz* is no more than workmanlike in construction—the story is told considerably better in the 1939 MGM film version than in the book—and the numerous sequels are largely reworkings of the same themes over and again, though they are told with pace and humour.[10]

According to Michael Patrick Hearn, the one authority to take an independent stand was the British John Rowe Townsend, who published the first edition of *Written for Children* in 1965 (Hearn 1983, xiii). A respected children's author, Townsend maintained that Baum

> has been shockingly underrated by American authorities on children's literature.... I cannot help wondering whether some unconscious snobbery was involved: a partiality for [Howard] Pyle, the cultured Easterner making use of Old World materials, contrasted with a feeling that fantasy was too lofty and refined a genre for a newspaperman from the Middle West.
>
> To an outsider it seems that the unabashed American-ness of the Oz books makes them all the more original and attractive.[11]

Townsend raises an interesting question: What really lies behind the condemnation of the Oz books? After hearing again and again how poorly written *The Wizard* is, it comes as a shock to pick up the actual book and discover that Baum's style, while not "distinguished," is not "flat and dull" either. As Edward Wagenknecht judiciously states in his second look at Baum in 1962, "[I]f he is not a stylist in the sense in which, say, Walter de la Mare is a stylist, there is still no excuse for failing to recognize that he wrote with admirable clarity and vigor and charm" (Hearn 1983, 159). In "Why Librarians Dislike Oz" (1962), Martin Gardner suggests several possible reasons, including a general disapproval of children's series for their poor literary quality, the expense of acquiring an entire series, and the specialization of Baum's publisher in poor-quality series books.[12] These arguments, too, are ultimately unconvincing. Some of the best children's books come in series, and the same librarians who banned the Oz books in the 1950s did not hesitate to purchase the Little House books, Arthur Ransome's Swallows and Amazons series, or the Doctor Dolittle books—or, for that matter, such popular though hardly classic series as Lucy Fitch Perkins's "Twins," Walter Farley's Black Stallion, or Walter R. Brooks's Freddy the Pig. Librarians could have restricted their Oz books to those written by Baum, if they felt that the post-Baum books were of lesser quality.

Townsend's surmise of cultural bias may be partially correct. But in her concern to raise the status and quality of children's books, Anne Carroll Moore may also have been troubled by the blatantly commercial aspect of Oz—the stage musicals, movies, publicity gimmicks, and spin-off games and toys. Such commodification of children's books was rare at that time, though it seems commonplace now. When it became clear, after Baum's death, that his publisher did not care whether Baum wrote the annual Oz book or not, this may have been Moore's last straw.[13] But just why the Oz books were originally blacklisted and why Moore's unilateral decision was adopted by generations of librarians is still a riddle for some researcher to unravel.

The 1960s witnessed a new and growing interest in popular fiction as a mirror of culture. Children's literature, too, was entering the academic world; seven scholarly journals devoted entirely to children's literature were founded between 1969 and 1977. As an icon of popular culture and a much-loved children's book, *The Wizard* attracted increasing scholarly attention. Today one can find analyses of *The Wizard* and the other Oz books from nearly every perspective imaginable, though the main (often overlapping) categories seem to be the literary historical, the sociopolitical (including analyses of Oz as utopia), the spiritual, and the psychological.

In "The Land of Oz: America's Great Good Place" (1970), Marius Bewley connects Baum to the mainstream of American literature. The tension between pastoralism and technology, he argues, is one of the main themes of American literature, and in Oz that tension is successfully resolved.[14] Brian Attebery's *Fantasy Tradition in American*

*Literature* (1980) places the Oz books in that tradition and explains in detail what makes them crucial to the history of American fantasy.

Several studies relate the Oz books to their context in American history. Jordan Brotman, in "A Late Wanderer in Oz" (1965), sees in them a number of traditional midwestern attitudes but also suggests that the theme of migration from Kansas to Oz reflects the real-life migration of Midwesterners—including Baum himself—to southern California.[15] Henry M. Littlefield stresses Baum's sympathy with the Midwestern Populist movement of the 1890s. In "The Wizard of Oz: Parable on Populism" (1964), he offers an ingenious allegorical interpretation in which the Scarecrow represents the exploited Midwestern farmer, the Tin Woodman the dehumanized factory worker, the Cowardly Lion William Jennings Bryan, and the Silver Shoes the elusive silver standard.[16] According to Fred Erisman, on the other hand, Baum's primary affinity is with the Progressive movement. He argues in "L. Frank Baum and the Progressive Dilemma" (1968) that Baum, like other Progressives, found difficulty in adapting his rural ideas of simplicity, individuality, industry, and generosity to an increasingly urbanized society, but that he expressed through the Oz books his hope that a younger generation might succeed in doing so.[17]

Some more recent scholars, however, pointing to Baum's career in decorating store windows, see the Oz books as harbingers of twentieth-century consumer culture. Stuart Culver calls Oz "Baum's Consumer Paradise" in "What Manikins Want: *The Wonderful Wizard of Oz* and *The Art of Decorating Dry Goods Windows*" (1988).[18] William Leach agrees, claiming in *Land of Desire: Merchants, Power, and the Rise of a New American Culture* (1993) that *The Wizard*, "far from challenging the new industrial society, endorsed its values and direction."[19] He links *The Wizard* with the popular philosophy of "mind cure," which denied the existence of genuine pain and suffering.

The majority of scholars with a sociopolitical perspective have taken a more positive view of Baum's utopia. S. J. Sackett, in "The Utopia of Oz" (1960), examines its value system in detail and sees there respect for individual freedom and nonconformity, the absence of militarism, equality of the sexes, a progressive view of prison reform, voluntary acceptance of responsibility, and "the need for the intellect and the emotions to be brought into harmony" (Hearn 1983, 220)—in short, virtually everything needed to ensure the continuance of democracy and civilization.[20] Jack Zipes's *Fairy Tales and the Art of Subversion* (1983) includes Baum among those nineteenth-century authors who subverted the fairy tale's traditional patterns of gender and class socialization and "expanded the fairy-tale discourse on civilization to conceive alternative worlds and styles of life."[21] His *Fairy Tale as Myth/Myth as Fairy Tale* (1994) further explores the interpretation of Oz as "everything America did not become" and examines two recent "utopian revisions" of the Oz myth, Philip Jose Farmer's *A Barnstormer in Oz* and Geoff Ryman's *Was*.[22]

Studies of gender and family in the Oz books also tend to see Baum as subverting or questioning traditional values. An influential 1974 article in *Ms.* magazine, "Munchkins, Ozophiles, and Feminists Too" by Noah Seaman and Barbara Seaman, pointed out that females tend to hold the power positions in Oz.[23] And Joel D. Chaston contrasts the film's emphasis on "home" with Baum's less sentimental attitude and the absence of traditional families throughout the Oz books.[24]

Other scholars have interpreted Oz in terms of mythical, spiritual, or psychological symbolism. In an amusing article in *Psychology Today*, "The Wizard of Oz behind the Couch," Sheldon Kopp suggests that the Wizard is a wise psychotherapist who knows that he is really a man, not a wizard, and who helps others solve their own problems.[25] Osmond Beckwith applies a Freudian interpretation to the first four Oz books in "The Oddness of Oz" (1976).[26] J. Karl Franson also interprets *The Wizard* as allegory, but with a religious rather than a psychological slant. In "From Vanity Fair to Emerald City: Baum's Debt to Bunyan" (1995), he draws many parallels between *The Wizard* and *Pilgrim's Progress,* suggesting the latter as one of Baum's main sources.[27] Paul Nathanson combines Jungian and religious analyses in *Over the Rainbow: "The Wizard of Oz" as a Secular Myth of America* (1991).[28] He suggests that both the film and the book recapitulate the Jungian individuation process on one level and the Christian process of fall and redemption on another. On a third level, the film has become a secular ritual for Americans that expresses the tension in their culture between Kansas and Oz—the pastoral and traditional versus the technological and futuristic. Michael Patrick Hearn's annotations in *The Annotated Wizard of Oz* (1973) also explore the possibilities of a Jungian interpretation.

One benefit of this multiplicity of interpretations has been increased respect for the Oz books. If a work of literature inspires so much scrutiny, from so many diverse perspectives, it is probably worth looking at. And though the old anti-Oz prejudice has not entirely withered away, the Oz books are back on the library shelves again—to be enjoyed by new generations of children.

# A READING

# 4

# The Road to the Emerald City

What was it about *The Wizard of Oz* and its successors that won them the faithful support of so many children and ex-children, and enabled these books to survive decades of persecution? Whereas librarians had trouble articulating what they found so objectionable about the Oz books, defenders have written vividly of themselves as children immersed in Baum's imaginary world. For it seems to have been a world rather than simply a story that captivated them.

In "Oz and the Fifth Criterion," C. Warren Hollister freely concedes that the Oz books are not outstanding when measured by the usual literary criteria of theme, characterization, plot, and style. Comparing *The Wizard* to Ursula K. Le Guin's much praised *A Wizard of Earthsea* (1968), he declares bluntly,

> Baum's *Wizard of Oz* doesn't measure up. It appears to have no underlying theme—no unity of conception. Its characterizations seem shallow. Dorothy has no inner problems, doesn't develop, doesn't grow. Oz never really changes. As for plot, it rambles. There is a pointless story within a story in Chapter 14, and the last seven chapters, involving a long journey to the Quadling country, are anticlimactic. The style, which has been described,

unfairly, as "sentimental" is, in fact, straightforward but undistinguished, lacking in sparkle and in witty, surprising turns of phrase. (Hearn 1983, 193)

Hollister probably overstates his case against *The Wizard*. Baum's characters may not be complex, but many of them—the Wizard himself, for example, and Dorothy's three companions—are original and memorable. And although other books in the series may lack an "underlying theme," Hollister's criticism certainly does not hold true for *The Wizard*. At least two themes are clear enough to be perceived even by children: Dorothy's quest demonstrates (as in many folktales) that persistence through all obstacles and dangers enables us to attain our goals, while the quest of her three companions suggests that the inner qualities we most desire—courage, intelligence, and a loving heart—can be found within ourselves.

It is fair to say, however, that Baum's characters do not change or grow; that the other Oz books, for the most part, do not develop strong underlying themes; that Baum's plots are rambling (much more so in some of his other books than in *The Wizard*); and that his style lacks literary distinction. How, then, to explain the lasting appeal of the Oz books?

Hollister proposes a "fifth criterion" by which to measure children's fantasy. "Three-dimensionality," as he calls it, is "the magical tugging of the child-reader through the page into the story—into the other world. You not only suspend disbelief in Oz; you not only positively, ardently believe in Oz; you are there!" Three-dimensionality produces "that beguilement, utterly transcending the four criteria, which brings joyous intoxication to the child-reader and, afterward, a memory that never passes—a recollection of the taste of joy, the three-dimensional experience of going into another universe where everything is brighter and more fragrant, more dangerous, and more alive" (Hearn 1983, 195).

Three-dimensionality, says Hollister, also helps to explain why the Oz books seem deficient in other literary criteria:

> Dorothy is superficial? Rather she is broadly sketched so that children can become Dorothy for a time.... Why aren't the Oz plots more unified? Real adventures in magical lands are, as children

know, tantalizingly open-ended. Why isn't Baum's style more glittering? Because glitter gets in the way. To pass through the page into the other world, the words must be as nearly *invisible* as possible.... Where is the theme? The theme is Oz. (Hearn 1983, 196)

Three-dimensionality, then, is the creation of an imaginary world so real and so appealing that it becomes irresistible to a susceptible reader. According to Hollister, C. S. Lewis's Narnia and J. R. R. Tolkien's Middle-earth share this quality (195). Of course, not all readers are susceptible; some critics have found the appeal of Oz (and of Narnia and Middle-earth, for that matter) essentially incomprehensible.

Hollister provides a good description of what children who love the Oz books experience, but he stops there. He does not attempt to explain how the three-dimensionality of Oz is created or—except for a few hints—how it works. In this study, I look for answers to these questions, exploring the creation, structural principles, significance, and appeal of Baum's imaginary world. Since most children today are introduced to *The Wizard* by the film version, a final chapter compares the imaginary world depicted in the film with Baum's concept of Oz.

The process that brings a literary work into being is often compared by the writers themselves to the gestation and birth of a baby. But if the baby's heredity is a mixture of genes from its two parents, at least three "parents" contribute "genes" to a work of literature. Literary influences, the personal experience and mind-set of the author, and the cultural-historical context in which the work is produced are all mingled in the new creation. Although these influences do not explain what is unique in the work—any more than the baby is simply the sum of its genes—they reveal a good deal about the mysterious process that brought it to life. *The Wizard of Oz* is a particularly interesting example, since most accounts of it, including Baum's own, have emphasized how different it was from the children's stories that had come before.

Baum's introduction reads like a kind of manifesto, in which he tries to distance *The Wizard* from the traditional fairy tales of Grimm and Andersen and proclaims it a "modernized fairy tale"—a new kind of children's story that will retain the "wonderment and joy" of the old fairy tales but will eliminate their "heart-aches and nightmares," their "blood-curdling" incidents "devised ... to point a fearsome moral," and their "stereotyped" supernatural characters (*Wizard*, 1). Nonetheless, as Russel B. Nye suggests, "The Oz books conform to the accepted pattern far more often than they deviate" (Gardner and Nye, 2). As we've seen, *The Wizard* is based on the ancient formula of the magical quest story, and although it includes such nontraditional characters as the Scarecrow and the Tin Woodman, it also makes free use of the witches and talking animals of the folktale. Many individual episodes, as well, are reminiscent of traditional stories. The episode in which the Queen of the Mice is saved from a wildcat by the Tin Woodman and gratefully rallies her people to drag the sleeping Lion from the Deadly Poppy Field echoes Aesop's fable of the Lion and the Mouse, as well as innumerable folktales in which grateful animals help the protagonist. And as in folktales, things tend to come in threes. Dorothy has three companions, she visits three countries in Oz, the magical Golden Cap can be used only three times by each owner, and the heels of the Silver Shoes are clicked together three times to make their magic work.

In 1909 Baum wrote an article entitled "Modern Fairy Tales"; besides the introduction to *The Wizard,* this is our main source of first-hand information on what he liked and disliked in the fantasies of other authors and what he aimed for in his own. Surveying the field historically from the folktale through Hans Christian Andersen and Lewis Carroll to the fantasies of his own generation, he mentions with approval such contemporary authors as Howard Pyle, E. Nesbit, and Frances Hodgson Burnett. Baum places a high value on "drollery," "imaginative power," cleverness, and entertainment.[1] What children look for, he says, is "action—'something doing every minute'—exciting adventures, unexpected difficulties to be overcome, and marvelous escapes"—all of which certainly characterize the Oz books. "To my mind," he declares, "a good book of this sort is just as necessary to the proper promotion of a child's welfare as baths, exercise, or wholesome food" (140). Good modern fairy tales "will feed the imaginative instinct of the little ones and develop the best side of child nature" (139).

On the other hand, says Baum, parents should avoid fairy tales that are "marred by murders or cruelties, by terrifying characters, or by mawkish sentimentality, love and marriage." The only specific story to receive a negative comment here is Dinah Maria Mulock's *Little Lame Prince* (1875), which Baum concedes is "charmingly written" but "too pitiful in sentiment" (Hearn 1983, 139). But those familiar with the full range of Victorian fairy tales can easily provide additional examples—stories like Lucy Clifford's terrifying "The New Mother," George MacDonald's gruesome "The Giant's Heart," and Christina Rossetti's nightmarish and moralistic *Speaking Likenesses*, which go well beyond the degree of violence and scariness Baum allowed in the Oz books. Some of Andersen's fairy tales also fit Baum's negative criteria; "The Red Shoes," "The Girl Who Trod on a Loaf," and "The Little Mermaid" are stories he may have had in mind.

It is not, however, Andersen's occasional cruelties, his moralizing, or his sentimentality that Baum specifically objects to in "Modern Fairy Tales," but his style. Baum praises Andersen wholeheartedly for his "marvelous imagination" and "beautiful descriptive passages" but believes that these passages are unsuited to children's tastes. "As children you skipped those passages—I can guess that, because as a child I skipped them myself—but as women you ought to read Andersen again, that you may revel in the beauties of his splendid descriptions, and enjoy the fascination of his poesy" (Hearn 1983, 138). Not surprisingly, Baum's own stories are notably free from lengthy descriptive passages.

What Baum did adopt from this great predecessor was one of Andersen's most striking innovations—his use of animated inanimate objects as individualized characters and even protagonists in their own right. Stories like "The Fir Tree," "The Staunch Tin Soldier," "The Darning Needle," and "The Top and the Ball" were hailed as something new in fantasy and widely imitated, though seldom with success. Baum, however, succeeded brilliantly in bringing to life not only the Scarecrow in *The Wizard* but numerous characters in later Oz books— the Sawhorse, the Patchwork Girl, the Gump, and many more.

The children's author from whom Baum learned most, however, was unquestionably Lewis Carroll. Despite obvious dissimilarities, the Alice books provided *The Wizard* with its basic premise: the adventures of an ordinary little girl who by chance finds her way from our real-life world to an imaginary one with inhabitants and natural laws differing markedly from ours, and who eventually returns home, apparently unchanged by her experience. Carroll's example must have encouraged Baum to give free rein to his wildly inventive imagination and his sense of humor. And the revolutionary absence of any moral whatsoever in the Alice books had set an invaluable precedent. "Modern education includes morality; therefore the modern child seeks only entertainment in its wonder-tales," Baum declares in his introduction to *The Wizard;* his story, like Carroll's, "was written solely to pleasure children of today" (2).

But what seems to have impressed Baum most about the Alice books, judging from "Modern Fairy Tales," was Alice herself. It seems "fair to state," says Baum,

> that the children loved Alice better than any prince or princess that Andersen ever created. The secret of Alice's success lay in the fact that she was a real child, and any normal child could sympathize with her all through her adventures. The story may often bewilder the little one—for it is bound to bewilder us, having neither plot nor motive in its relation—but Alice is doing something every moment, and doing something strange and marvelous, too; so the child follows her with rapturous delight. (Hearn 1983, 138)

Baum's Dorothy, too, is a "real child" who is "doing something every moment," though Baum was careful to provide her adventures with the clear plot and motivation that were missing from the "rambling and incoherent" *Alice in Wonderland* (139).

Two minor yet interesting resemblances between the Alice books and *The Wizard* confirm the strength of Carroll's influence on Baum. One of these is the physical size of the heroine. Although Alice undergoes several disconcerting changes of size in Wonderland, she succeeds eventually in making herself the same size as the "adult" characters; she is also the same size as the "adults" in the Looking-Glass Country. This holds true for Dorothy as well. The first inhabitants of Oz she encounters, the Munchkins, "seemed about as tall as Dorothy, who was a well-grown child for her age" (12). In both cases, equality of size helps to give the child-protagonist equal status in the new world.[2] And both *Through the Looking-Glass* and *The Wizard* end with extremely short chapters, as Alice and Dorothy abruptly return home. The great difference here, of course, is that Dorothy's magical adventures, unlike Alice's, are not mere dreams. Unlike Carroll's imaginary worlds—and unlike the Oz of the MGM movie—Baum's Oz is not an illusion but a reality.

Whereas Carroll's influence on *The Wizard* was apparent even to Baum's earliest reviewers, the possible influence of an important American children's author has gone largely unnoticed. In the late nineteenth century, Frank Stockton was probably the best-known writer of fairy tales in America and, more to the point, the first writer to give his fairy tales a consistently American flavor. His settings and characters are more European than Baum's; his small kingdoms are the familiar quasi-medieval variety, while his supernatural creatures are collected from folklore and myth—wizards, dwarfs, giants, fairies, sphinxes, genies, gnomes, griffins, and dryads, all mixed together. Baum uses a far higher proportion of invented creatures, and protagonists like Dorothy, being from our world, don't take them for granted as Stockton's princes and princesses tend to do. What seems distinctively American in the works of both authors is the way in which these assorted creatures can mingle and coexist in harmony. Fairyland is multiethnic and, despite the princes and princesses, essentially democratic; a conspicuous difference between Oz and Wonderland is the absence in Oz of the unpleasant class and status games played constantly in Wonderland. Even the oddest of Baum's creatures has its "rights" and assumes equality with the rest. The matter-of-factness with which Baum presents them, and their simple, colloquial American speech may also owe something to Stockton's example. As Stockton himself explained his approach to fantasy,

> I caused the fanciful creatures who inhabited the world of fairy-land to act, as far as possible for them to do so, as if they were inhabitants of the real world. I did not dispense with monsters and enchanters, or talking beasts and birds, but I obliged these creatures to infuse into their extraordinary actions a certain leaven of common sense.[3]

Another characteristic shared by Stockton and Baum—and typically nineteenth-century American—is their delight in inventions and mechanical devices. Baum clearly enjoys the ingenuity of the Wizard's illusions and describes in detail how the Wizard and Dorothy made their hot-air balloon. Tik-Tok, the clockwork man introduced in *Ozma of Oz,* has been called the first true robot in fiction; he can think and speak but runs down periodically and must be rewound.[4] He may have been directly inspired by the mechanical city in Stockton's "How the Aristocrats Sailed Away," a city whose inhabitants periodically fall asleep until someone winds it up again. Several of Stockton's stories revolve around ingenious inventions—some possible, like "The Tricycle of the Future," others pure fantasy, like "My Translataphone."

Baum may also have acquired from Stockton a basic narrative strategy that can be found not only in *The Wizard* but in many of his later Oz books. Whereas in both Alice books, Alice travels alone and is often lonely, Dorothy is soon joined by the oddly assorted companions who become her close friends. Similarly, several of Stockton's fairy tales feature a naive protagonist who journeys through strange lands, meeting a succession of odd yet friendly creatures who often join the traveling party. Baum refers specifically to one of these stories in "Modern Fairy Tales"; "Frank Stockton," he says, "wrote a most bewitching story of the good class called 'The Floating Prince' " (Hearn 1983, 139). The prince, Nassime, has lost his kingdom to a usurper and sets off to found a new one, deciding that "[t]he first person I meet shall be my chief councilor of state, the second shall be head of the army, the third shall be admiral of the navy, the next shall be chief treasurer, and then I will collect subjects of various classes."[5] The first "person" is a diminutive fairy, who nonetheless makes a fine chief councilor; a giant, a shepherd on stilts, and a clam-digger become Nassime's general, admiral, and treasurer; a class of schoolboys becomes his aristocracy; and a caravan of rich merchants and philosophers, his common people. The fairy finds a place for Nassime's kingdom, and they all settle down happily together (except the schoolboys—but that is another story). If Baum found "The Floating Prince" "bewitching," he may well have adapted its structure for his own purposes.

Children's authors are by no means isolated from what is happening in literature for adults; current developments—especially in

Chicago—also played a part in the creation of *The Wizard.* Michael Patrick Hearn has suggested that Hamlin Garland, the Chicago novelist known as "the Ibsen of the West," may have influenced both Baum's introduction and his opening chapter (1973, 85, 93). Garland's famous essay "The Emancipation of the West" (1893) had called for a rejection of European literary forms and for the creation of new, indigenous forms by Midwestern authors; he named his own harshly realistic portrayals of the Midwest "Veritism"—realism with a strong regional flavor. Baum's announcement that "the time has come for a series of newer 'wonder tales'' ' may have been intended to do for children's fantasy what Garland had done with his "Emancipation" essay. Chapter 1 of *The Wizard,* with its drought-stricken landscape and homesteading family grimly struggling for existence, is a beginning straight from a Veritist novel—though the rest of the story could not have been what Garland had in mind.

Although Baum may have supported the aims of Veritism, his natural bent lay in a very different direction. In the late nineteenth century, utopian novels provided an alternative venue for social criticism—one more congenial to Baum's hopeful temperament. More than 60 such visions of ideal societies were published in America between 1888 and 1900 (Baum and MacFall, 124). The most famous of these was Edward Bellamy's *Looking Backward, 2000–1887,* which Baum himself had playfully parodied in the "Our Landlady" column of his Aberdeen newspaper (Hearn 1973, 18). Bellamy's protagonist falls into a kind of trance in the year 1887 and wakes to find himself in the wonderfully transformed Boston of 2000. Crime, war, class struggle, poverty, and money have disappeared under a form of democratic socialism called "Nationalism," in which the government is the only employer. Everyone does an equal share of work in the "industrial army" and shares equally in the abundant economy, retiring at the age of 45. Technological advances emphasize the socialistic nature of this utopia; when it rains in Boston, the sidewalks are automatically covered with a continuous protective awning. A character observes that "in the nineteenth century, when it rained, the people of Boston put up three hundred thousand umbrellas over as many heads, and in the twentieth century they put up one umbrella over all the heads."[6]

Baum, who liked inventions, would surely have appreciated this one. Although he did not fully develop the utopian aspect of Oz until he had written several Oz books, even *The Wizard* depicts a world whose inhabitants—save those enslaved by evil witches—seem universally contented and free from economic anxiety. In the Emerald City, for example, "Everyone seemed happy and contented and prosperous" (118). At this point, however—perhaps under the American Wizard's influence?—Oz is still operating on a money economy. Dorothy notices "many shops" in the city streets and children paying for their green lemonade with green pennies (202). By 1910 and *The Emerald City of Oz,* Baum had worked out the details of an imaginary economy that—if one substitutes the fairy ruler Ozma for the American government—seems much like Bellamy's:

> Altogether there were more than half a million people in the Land of Oz—although some of them, as you will soon learn, were not made of flesh and blood as we are—and every inhabitant of that favored country was happy and prosperous.
>
> No disease of any sort was ever known among the Ozites, and so no one ever died unless he met with an accident that prevented him from living. This happened very seldom, indeed. There were no poor people in the Land of Oz, because there was no such thing as money, and all property of every sort belonged to the Ruler. The people were her children, and she cared for them. Each person was given freely by his neighbors whatever he required for his use, which is as much as any one may reasonably desire. Some tilled the lands and raised great crops of grain, which was divided equally among the entire population, so that all had enough. There were many tailors and dressmakers and shoemakers and the like, who made things that any who desired them might wear. Likewise there were jewelers who made ornaments for the person, which pleased and beautified the people, and these ornaments also were free to those who asked for them. Each man and woman, no matter what he or she produced for the good of the community, was supplied by the neighbors with food and clothing and a house and furniture and ornaments and games. If by chance the supply ever ran short, more was taken from the great storehouses of the Ruler, which were afterward filled up again when there was more of any article than the people needed.

> Every one worked half the time and played half the time, and
> the people enjoyed the work as much as they did the play, because
> it is good to be occupied and to have something to do.[7]

"I do not suppose such an arrangement would be practical with us," Baum comments sardonically, "but Dorothy assures me that it works finely with the Oz people" (31).

Unlike Bellamy's, however, Baum's utopia is essentially rural rather than urban. The Emerald City (with a population of 57,318) is his only big city, and even its environs are "full of pretty and comfortable farmhouses, in which resided those inhabitants of Oz who preferred country to city life" (*Emerald,* 30). In many ways, his utopia seems more akin to that of British socialist William Morris, who called Bellamy's vision of a regimented, urbanized, technological future "a horrible cockney dream."[8]

The narrator of Morris's utopia, *News from Nowhere* (1891), is a London socialist who wakes one morning to find himself (like Bellamy's narrator) in the wonderful twenty-first century. As an artist who cared deeply for the beauty of the natural world, Morris was more interested in depicting a beautiful, happy, rural society than in the practical questions of how to achieve it. He describes the colorful, comfortable clothes—inspired by medieval clothing—that his people wear, how they spend their time, what their buildings look like, and even what they have for breakfast, but he passes over why their population density is so low, how their economy sustains itself, and what technology might make all this possible.

Baum got some practical ideas from Bellamy, substituting magic for Bellamy's technology; the enchantment that lies on Oz also solved his population problem by eliminating birth, aging, and natural death (as he explains in more detail in *The Tin Woodman of Oz*).[9] But Morris may have helped him visualize what a really appealing ideal society might look and feel like:

> Both shores had a line of very pretty houses, low and not large,
> standing back a little way from the river; they were mostly built
> of red brick and roofed with tiles, and looked, above all, comfort-
> able, and as if they were, so to say, alive and sympathetic with the

life of the dwellers in them. There was a continuous garden in front of them, going down to the water's edge, in which the flowers were now blooming luxuriantly, and sending delicious waves of summer scent over the eddying stream.[10]

This might be a more descriptive version of the Emerald City's environs, where "[h]andsome houses stood on both sides of the road and each had a green lawn before it as well as a pretty flower garden."[11]

One of the most striking aspects of the future, to Morris's protagonist, is how different people's faces look than they did in the late nineteenth century:

Almost everybody was gaily dressed, but especially the women.... Some faces I saw that were thoughtful, and in these I noticed great nobility of expression, but none that had a glimmer of unhappiness, and the greater part (we came upon a good many people) were frankly and openly joyous. (Morris, 201)

This device is one that Baum used repeatedly, beginning with *The Wizard:* everyone in the Emerald City "seemed happy and contented and prosperous" (118). A more elaborate description, even more like Morris's, appears in Baum's description of the City in *The Road to Oz:*

There were many people on these walks—men, women, and children—all dressed in handsome garments of silk or satin or velvet, with beautiful jewels. Better even than this: all seemed happy and contented, for their faces were smiling and free from care, and music and laughter might be heard on every side.[12]

Again, as the travelers approached the Emerald City in *The Patchwork Girl of Oz,* "[T]hey met a good many people who were coming or going from one place or another. All these seemed happy-faced, pleasant people, who nodded graciously to the strangers as they passed, and exchanged words of greeting" (186). This welcoming attitude toward strangers is also a feature of Morris's utopia. Frank Joslyn Baum and Russell P. MacFall, who first noted the influence of Bellamy and Morris on Baum in their biography of Baum, *To Please a Child,* point out that "[l]ike Oz, Morris's England is an uncomplicated land of small farms and villages" and call attention to "an incident in *News from Nowhere* which might have come right out of Ozma's kingdom" (201):

> We came just here on a gang of men road mending. . . . They were laughing and talking merrily with each other and the women, but presently their foreman looked up and saw our way stopped. So he stayed his pick and sang out, "Spell ho, mates! here are neighbours wanting to get past." Whereupon the others stopped also, and drawing around us, helped the old horse by easing our wheels over the half undone road, and then, like men with a pleasant task on hand, hurried back to their work, only stopping to give us a smiling good-day. (Morris, 222–23)

In Oz, too, Baum tells us, "[P]eople enjoyed the work as much as they did the play."

If Baum learned from Morris something of how to create an appealing utopia, however, it was thoroughly assimilated. Morris's richly descriptive, slightly archaic language in these passages is utterly different from the colloquial simplicity of Baum's, and the feel of Baum's utopia is as American as Morris's is British.

The relationship of Baum's utopia to those of Bellamy and Morris seems to bear out Marius Bewley's suggestion in "The Land of Oz: America's Great Good Place" that the Oz books represent a creative solution to the tension between the pastoral and the technological. Under Ozma's rule, magic-technology is, as Bewley puts it, "under the control of the central government"; that is, only Ozma, Glinda, and the Wizard (who, after his return to Oz, becomes Glinda's apprentice) are legally permitted to practice it (Hearn 1983, 205). Thus, Oz can remain a pastoral utopia while enjoying the benefits of a highly developed technology. The outcome of *The Wizard* helps to ensure that magic will no longer be practiced by those who would use it for evil ends, like the Wicked Witches, or who only pretend to know what they are doing with it, like the humbug Wizard prior to his apprenticeship with Glinda; eliminating these unworthy practitioners clears the ground for Ozma's sweeping reforms. It seems that Baum studied

The Wizard, in John R. Neill's illustration, bears distinct resemblance to the showman P. T. Barnum.
*From* The Patchwork Girl of Oz *(Chicago: Reilly and Britton, 1913).*

carefully the alternatives represented by Bellamy and Morris and came up with a solution that allowed Oz the best of both.[13]

But Frank Baum's childhood memories and his years in Aberdeen and Chicago were at least as influential in that creation as anything he had ever read. We know, for example, that the character of the Scarecrow came straight from his childhood. "When I was a boy I was tremendously interested in scarecrows," he told an interviewer for the Philadelphia *North American* in 1904. "They always seemed to my childish imagination as just about to wave their arms, straighten up and stalk across the field on their long legs. I lived on a farm, you know."[14] According to the Baum-MacFall biography, Baum had recurring nightmares of being chased by these animated scarecrows. "Happily, Frank always dashed away while the scarecrow waddled after him and finally collapsed into a pile of shapeless straw" (22). It seems typical of Baum, with his desire to expunge "heart-aches and nightmares" from children's fantasy, that he should have transformed his own nightmare into something harmless and even lovable.

The single most important childhood influence in the creation of Oz was Rose Lawn, the beautiful country estate where Baum grew up. More than one commentator has read his description of Rose Lawn (scarcely disguised as "Roselawn") in *Dot and Tot of Merryland* (1901) and been reminded of Dorothy's first sight of Oz, with its "lovely patches of green sward," "stately trees," and "banks of gorgeous flowers" (*Wizard*, 100):

> The cool but sun-kissed mansion seemed delightful after the formal city house. It was built in a quaint but pretty fashion, and with many wings and gables and broad verandas on every side. Before it were acres and acres of velvety green lawns, sprinkled with shrubbery and dotted with beds of bright flowers. In every direction were winding paths covered with white gravel, which led to all parts of the grounds, looking for all the world like a map. (Hearn 1973, 12)

This was Baum's childhood world, for he was educated at home by private tutors. Small wonder if he looked back on it as a kind of Paradise—all the more so because, like Adam, he had been forcibly cast out of it, not once but twice. At 12, he was sent to Peekskill Military Academy; his first experience of school, where bullying teachers and the totally regimented life gave him a lasting dislike of the military, was a brutal contrast to the sheltered, leisured existence he had always known. When he was allowed to return to Rose Lawn two years later, after a severe illness, it was as though he had his childhood back again. The years that other young men spent studying in college or working at their first real jobs Baum devoted to pursuing his favorite hobbies and daydreams—editing an amateur newspaper (a common children's hobby in the late nineteenth century), breeding fancy chickens, and acting the lead roles in his own plays. Even marriage and fatherhood did not end his financial dependence on his father or his ties with the family home. Then came his father's death and the collapse of the family fortunes. Rose Lawn was sold, and this time Baum had lost his childhood Paradise for good. Only by creating in his imagination a new world full of trees and lawns and flower gardens—a world preserved from change by magic—could he return there.

Rose Lawn must have seemed even greener and more beautiful in contrast with the dry, treeless prairies of the Midwest, where Frank and Maud emigrated after the family disaster. And their new home, Aberdeen, sinking inexorably into depression after years of crop failures, and dragging Baum's Bazaar and his weekly newspaper down with it, brought the Baums only hardship, anxiety, and failure. Baum's bleak picture of Kansas in the opening chapter of *The Wizard* is clearly based less on the principles of Veritism than on grim personal experience. By the time he created Oz, however, his fortunes had improved; thanks to his own talents and exertions, he had a comfortable home in Chicago, a successful business enterprise, and a promising career as a writer. With Aberdeen 10 years behind him, he could place his experience in perspective and use it with calculated effect. The devastating tornadoes—one had hit Aberdeen in 1890 (Carpenter and Shirley, 37)—became a new and exciting way to transport a character from one world to another. And the contrast between Aberdeen and Rose Lawn was translated into the contrast between Kansas and Oz. Oz (like Rose Lawn) seems even greener and more beautiful set against the gray sterility and deprivation of Kansas, and the moment when

Dorothy opens the door of her Kansas home and steps out into Oz is a high point of Baum's fantasy.

When he left Aberdeen for Chicago in 1891, Baum also took with him a sympathetic understanding of the Midwest's hard-pressed farmers, an understanding that he could never have attained as a rich man's son at Rose Lawn. Not coincidentally, his only involvement in politics occurred in the turbulent 1890s, when agrarian discontent came to a head. The first convention of the farmers' People's Party was held in Topeka, Kansas, where the fiery suffragist Mary Elizabeth Lease told her audience, "What you farmers need to do is to raise less corn and more *Hell*!" When a two-year depression hit the country in 1893, bringing lowered grain prices, farm foreclosures, strikes, and riots in its wake, Populists joined with members of both parties in an attempt to make more money available by abandoning the gold standard and coining silver. The question of gold versus silver became the key issue, pitting creditors against debtors, rich against poor. No one living in Chicago could escape the turmoil and controversy of the times; Baum was there in 1894, when federal troops were sent in to contain the Pullman Strike, setting off an explosion of mob violence. In 1896 William Jennings Bryan was nominated by the Democratic Party on a platform of unlimited coinage of silver and gold. Baum became a Bryan supporter, marching for his candidate in torchlight parades through the streets of Chicago. After Bryan lost the election to William McKinley that fall, Baum never again showed signs of political activism.

Henry M. Littlefield has suggested in "The Wizard of Oz: Parable on Populism" that Baum's story is actually a Populist allegory in which Dorothy's Silver Shoes represent the magical power of silver coinage. Although the article was written largely tongue-in-cheek, it does make an interesting point about the Wizard, who, says Littlefield, "might be any president from Grant to McKinley ... [H]e symbolizes the American criterion for leadership—he is able to be everything to everybody" (228). Essentially, however, he is a humbug—able to solve imaginary problems, like the Scarecrow's, but helpless in the face of real ones, like Dorothy's. Perhaps the Wizard does represent Baum's disillusionment with American politics and presidents.

Baum never lost his compassion for the struggling Midwestern farmers and their wives, however, or his generous indignation on their behalf, which lends force to his portraits of Dorothy's Aunt Em and Uncle Henry:

> When Aunt Em came there to live she was a young, pretty wife. The sun and wind had changed her, too. They had taken the sparkle from her eyes and left them a sober gray; they had taken the red from her cheeks and lips, and they were gray also. She was thin and gaunt, and never smiled, now. . . .
>
> Uncle Henry never laughed. He worked hard from morning till night and did not know what joy was. He was gray also, from his long beard to his rough boots, and he looked stern and solemn, and rarely spoke. (*Wizard*, 8)

Like the farms near Aberdeen, Uncle Henry's land is suffering from prolonged drought: "The sun had baked the plowed land into a gray mass, with little cracks running through it. Even the grass was not green, for the sun had burned the tops of the long blades until they were the same gray color to be seen everywhere" (8). In Oz, the greenness of the countryside and prosperity of the farms becomes an immediate point of contrast between the two worlds. As the farm girl from Kansas begins her journey, for example, she is "surprised . . . to see how pretty the country was about her. There were neat fences at the sides of the road, painted a dainty blue color, and beyond them were fields of grain and vegetables in abundance" (19).

The connection between Baum's Populist sympathies and the Oz books is even more evident in *The Emerald City of Oz* (1910). Uncle Henry's plight has worsened, and it is now clear that the economic system may be as much to blame as the years of drought:

> It was not a big farm, nor a very good one, because sometimes the rain did not come when the crops needed it, and then everything withered and dried up. Once a cyclone had carried away Uncle Henry's house, so that he was obliged to build another; and as he was a poor man he had to mortgage his farm to get the money to pay for the new house. . . .

Uncle Henry grew poorer every year, and the crops raised on the farm only bought food for the family. Therefore the mortgage could not be paid. At last the banker who had loaned him the money said that if he did not pay on a certain day, his farm would be taken away from him.

This worried Uncle Henry a good deal, for without the farm he would have no way to earn a living. He was a good man, and worked in the fields as hard as he could; and Aunt Em did all the housework, with Dorothy's help. Yet they did not seem to get along. (21–22)

Baum finds no solution for Uncle Henry in Kansas. Instead, Dorothy gets Ozma's permission to bring the old couple to the Emerald City, and all three become permanent citizens of Oz. Later in this same book Baum presents the detailed description of Oz's utopian economic system; since this was intended to be the last book in the series and ends with Oz cut off from any communication with our world, we can assume that Baum meant to leave his readers with this vision of an ideal place where hunger and grinding poverty cannot exist.

Historical events, as well as Baum's personal experience, thus influenced his creation of Oz as a utopia; for him it seems to have represented not only a return to Rose Lawn but a visionary alternative to the human misery he had witnessed. But Baum's is not (unlike William Morris's) a purely rural utopia. There is a city at its center—not the drab, scientific Boston of *Looking Backward* but a city as glowing and colorful as a green jewel. Where did Baum find inspiration for this aspect of Oz? It seems likely that the main real-life source for Baum's Emerald City was the Chicago World's Fair of 1893.

The world's fairs of the nineteenth and early twentieth centuries, beginning with Prince Albert's dream child, the Great Exhibition of 1851, were intended not only to enhance national prestige but to sum up the best of modern civilization and encourage peace and prosperity throughout the world. Chicago's was the first ever held in the United States. The World's Columbian Exposition, as it was officially called, celebrated the 400th anniversary of Columbus's discovery of America; it was also meant to show the world that America had attained the heights of European civilization. Chicago was particularly eager to prove that the "Phoenix City," almost totally destroyed by fire in 1871, was now the equal of any on the East Coast. Serious planning began in 1890—around the same time that Baum moved to Chicago from Aberdeen—and despite the depression that engulfed the country in 1893, the city was able to come up with the $22 million needed to host the largest fair in history. The Chicago fairgrounds extended over 600 acres—compared to the 20 acres of the 1851 Crystal Palace; the 173 acres of the most recent world's fair, held at Paris in 1889; and the 236 acres of the Philadelphia Centennial Exhibition of 1876. Over 80 nations and colonies participated, a greater number than ever before in world's fair history. People had wondered whether visitors would come all the way from the East Coast, let alone Europe, to a frontier city like Chicago. But although the fair lasted only six months, it drew a record-breaking 27 million visitors—nearly half as many as the entire population of the United States.

The real impact of the Chicago Fair, however, lay not in these statistics but in the sense of sheer wonder it inspired. Impressed by the architectural unity of the Paris Fair, the Chicago World's Fair committee had conceived their own fair as a giant work of art. The great landscape architect Frederick Law Olmsted had been hired to design the master plan, and under his direction 600 acres of marshy lakeshore were transformed into a network of lakes, bridges, and canals. Fountains played; sailboats, Venetian gondolas, and noiseless electric launches flitted across the water; and along the shores of the two lakes towered magnificent buildings in the Beaux Arts style based on the architecture of Greece and Rome, all painted a dazzling snowy white. This, the core of the fair, became known as the White City; to adorn it, murals and statues were commissioned from some of the best artists in the country. Farther inland were the buildings representing other states and foreign countries in a medley of styles, and farther still the confusion of the Midway—"the lighter and more fantastic side of the Fair"[15]—with the first and largest Ferris wheel ever built. But the White City was what people remembered best. *A Week at the Fair,* the official guidebook, promised that "a visit to the Exposition ... will be one to cherish as the great event of a lifetime" (27), and for many the fair seems to have been nothing less. The White City was compared to Fairyland, and to the Celestial City in Bunyan's *Pilgrim's Progress*. Frances Hodgson Burnett wrote a book called *Two Little Pilgrims' Progress: A Story of the City Beautiful* (1895) about two children whose dream is to see the wonders of the fair, and how that dream changes their lives. Henry Adams sat on the steps of the Electricity Building, pondering the new technology that lit the White City after dark with millions of lights; later he devoted an entire chapter in *The Education of Henry Adams* (1907) to his fortnight at the fair.

Descriptions scarcely capture what must have been a truly magical experience. Major Ben C. Truman, the fair's official historian, takes the reader on an imaginary gondola ride around the Grand Basin:

> But fancy one's self on the scene, gondola included, after dark, the cooling breezes from the lake ruffling the water and fanning the cheek and the gorgeous *fete de nuit* in full progress! All the surrounding buildings are ablaze with opalescent light. The basin is necklaced with a double string of brilliants, and the domes, the arches, the pinnacles, the turrets, the pavilion roofs and angles stand out against the sable mantle of night in golden chains of luminous glory. The gilded dome of the Administration building at first seems a floating crown of a myriad of diamonds, then rests upon an iridescent pillow fringed with strung jewels and beads of fire.... All the while the search lights have been traversing the heavens; now shooting far across the lake and picking out a tiny sailboat; now lighting upon the airy Diana; emblazoning the statue of the Republic and adding glory to the fountain.... Many of the gondoliers have fine voices, and the mellow cadence of their dulcet love songs, accompanied by the melodious twang of the guitar or mandolin fill the air with sweet melody. On a moonlight night or in the luminous glow of electric illumination, one seems to be gliding on to an enchanted land on the rhythmical flow of song.[16]

*A Week at the Fair* describes a daylight voyage in language that combines the sensory with the spiritual:

> Gently gliding over the smooth crystal waters of the sunny lagoon, at every turn some new beauty bursts upon the enrap-

tured view and sinks deep into the soul. Glorious vistas, filled with visions of transcendent loveliness, open up in a shifting panorama of antique sculptures, palatial architecture, and tones of color that may be conceived in fancy, but which can never be told in cold prose. Drifting idly along and abandoning himself to the sensuousness of the hour, on every side surrounded by sights of beauty, it seems no extravagance to say that nothing short of the "New Jerusalem" can present more entrancing scenery, and only a vision of its glories can surpass the perfect beauty of those to be enjoyed on this trip. A feeling of sadness steals into the soul in connection with the deep draughts of beauty and sensuous ease, for he realizes that where to-day stand sparkling fountain and gilded dome, Moorish minarets, statues, and golden portals, in six months will be a deserted stretch of low-lying ground and wide reaches of storm-tossed lake.... Lie back in your gondola of faraway, old-time Venice ... for only a very few times in a long life may such a perfection of pleasures to all the senses be enjoyed. (184)

The knowledge that all this beauty would soon vanish added to the dreamlike quality of the fair. Never intended to be permanent, the buildings and outdoor statues had been constructed of wooden frames covered with "staff," a mixture of plaster strengthened with jute fibers and cement. Even the smallest pavilions of the fair would be considered architectural treasures today, had they survived, but only one building was chosen for permanent preservation: the Fine Arts Building was reconstructed in stronger materials and became Chicago's Museum of Science and Industry.

One important innovation of the Chicago World's Fair was its willingness to involve women in the planning process. It was the first world's fair to have a Board of Lady Managers—117 women drawn from every state in the Union, headed by Chicago's own Mrs. Potter Palmer. In addition to ensuring that women's achievements would be included side by side with those of men in all the major buildings, the women lobbied successfully for a building of their own—the first official world's fair exhibition planned and created entirely by women. Designed by Sophia Hayden, the first female architect to graduate from the Massachusetts Institute of Technology, the Woman's Building was decorated with statues, tapestries, and paintings by women artists (including a mural by Mary Cassatt) and filled with examples of women's achievements from all over the world. Not only a beautiful and brilliant social leader but a staunch feminist, Mrs. Potter Palmer opened the building to enthusiastic applause, speaking forcefully on the rights of all women to education and to work for equal pay. "Freedom and justice for all," she declared, "are infinitely more to be desired than pedestals for a few" (Truman, 179).[17]

Like most citizens of Chicago, Baum probably visited the world's fair many times; with his love of beauty and fantasy, it must have appealed greatly to him. One Baum family story actually takes place at the Woman's Building, where Frank had planned to meet Maud and their two older sons for lunch, not knowing that a banquet was being given there in honor of Eulalia, Infanta of Spain. When he arrived, he was unable to find Maud and the boys in the huge crowd clustered around the building, so he joined a procession entering the hall and sat down with the rest at the banquet table. As his son Harry told the story,

> Making the best of the situation, he was enjoying himself among his companions when some compelling force drew his attention to the balcony surrounding the reception area. And there, pressed tightly against the rail with a small child clutching either hand, was a tired and hungry mother staring at him in amazement and anger! (Carpenter and Shirley, 43)

Perhaps Frank and Maud had chosen the Woman's Building for lunch because of their mutual interest in women's issues. Maud, the daughter of a famous female suffragist, was a strong feminist herself, while Frank had championed women's rights in his Aberdeen newspaper. His imaginary world of Oz, as many have noticed, is one in which girls and women hold the positions of power; Ozma and Glinda, especially, are held up as models of a good ruler.[18] Could the beautiful and queenly Glinda have been based, in part, on Mrs. Potter Palmer?

A number of resemblances between the White City of Chicago and the Emerald City of Oz suggest how the former may have inspired the latter. Most significant was the magical quality both cities shared;

firsthand accounts suggest that visiting the White City was as close as one could come in real life to visiting the enchanted city of a fairy tale. The sense of entering another world was enhanced by the location of the fair; instead of being located within city limits, like the Paris Fair of 1889, the Chicago Fair was an hour's journey by cable car (or 15 minutes by train) from downtown, effectively separating it from the city. The swiftness with which the White City took form and the swiftness with which it disappeared when the fair was over added to the magic—almost as though the fair had been both created and removed with the wave of a wizard's wand.

Baum might have conceived of a single-colored city on his own, but the White City must have helped him imagine it more vividly. The glittering spectacle of the City at night was especially memorable. Accounts like Truman's describe buildings outlined with strings of jewel-like lights and the Columbian Fountain in the Court of Honor lit with changing, multicolored beams of light. Baum's Emerald City glows and glitters, too. As Dorothy and her friends approach it for the first time, they see "a beautiful green glow in the sky just before them" (*Wizard*, 61). Inside, the jewel-studded City is even brighter:

> Even with eyes protected by the green spectacles Dorothy and her friends were at first dazzled by the brilliancy of the wonderful City. The streets were lined with beautiful houses all built of green marble and studded everywhere with sparkling emeralds. They walked over a pavement of the same green marble, and where the blocks were joined together were rows of emeralds, set closely, and glittering in the brightness of the sun. (62–63)

The Emerald City, unlike the White City, is surrounded by a wall; there are gates at the four points of the compass, with the Royal Palace at the City's center (*Patchwork*, 184)—suggesting a miniature replica of Oz itself. But the general impression Baum gives of the Emerald City's architecture does resemble the buildings of the White City. Truman mentions how "the domes, the arches, the pinnacles, the turrets, the pavilion roofs and angles stand out against the sable mantle of night." *A Week at the Fair* speaks of "sparkling fountain and gilded dome, Moorish minarets, statues, and golden portals." In *The*

*Wizard,* as Dorothy and her friends turn for a last look at the Emerald City, "All they could see was a mass of towers and steeples behind the green walls, and high up above everything the spires and dome of the Palace of Oz" (114). Another distant view, in *The Road to Oz,* mentions "the magnificent spires and splendid domes of the superb city, sparkling like brilliant jewels as they towered above the emerald walls" (181). Again, in *The Patchwork Girl of Oz,* Baum tells us that "beyond the wall was the vast city it surrounded, and hundreds of jeweled spires, domes and minarets, flaunting flags and banners, reared their crests far above the towers of the gateways" (184). The domes and minarets are a striking architectural similarity between the White City and the Emerald City—since neither American nor European cities have such features—as are the "flags and banners." Illustrations of the Chicago Fair buildings show flags and banners fluttering everywhere—just as in Baum's description of the Royal Palace in *The Magic of Oz:* "From a hundred towers and domes floated the banners of Oz."[19] Even the absence of horses in both cities may be significant in an era when horse-drawn traffic was taken for granted. Despite the MGM movie's Horse of a Different Color, Baum notes in *The Wizard* that "[t]here seemed to be no horses nor animals of any kind; the men carried things around in little green carts, which they pushed before them" (63). For reasons of cleanliness, horses were barred from the White City as well; people walked or moved by boat through the network of canals.

In addition to these tangible details, there are more subtle resemblances between the White City and the Emerald City of Oz. The White City proclaimed that there need be no conflict between what was beautiful and traditional and what was new and scientific; the latest technology, electricity, was used to adorn buildings and public spaces inspired by those of Greece and Rome. Baum, too, was to incorporate technology into a world of traditional fairy magic, with inventions like Ozma's Magic Picture and mechanical characters like the Tin Woodman and Tik-Tok. As Russel B. Nye points out, "In the Oz books he expanded the resources of the fairy tale to include, for the first time, the mechanical developments of the 20th century.... Baum, in a burst of inspiration, moved the machine into the child's

Detail of the Fisheries Building at the 1893 World's Columbian Exposition; flags flying from every tower were typical of the White City.
*From* A Week at the Fair *(Chicago: Rand McNally, 1893).*

world of imagination, endowed it with life and magic, and made it the ally of all the forces of good and justice and well-being in Oz" (Gardner and Nye, 7). Again, by adopting the traditional architectural forms of European civilization, the White City suggested that America had successfully assimilated that civilization and (literally) filled those forms with achievements of its own. Baum took the traditional European form of the fairy tale and used it to express his own distinctly American values and ideas.

Finally, and perhaps most importantly, the White City was a kind of real-life utopia that proved—however briefly—the power of the visionary. For everyone who visited the fair, it was a revelation of what an ideal city might be if city builders consciously worked together to make something beautiful—a revelation, some even felt, with the potential to change American values for the better. In her architectural review of the fair, M. G. Van Rensselaer declared,

> No man or woman will come to Chicago this summer without recognizing that the Fair has been based on a serious recognition of the fact that commercial prosperity alone can not make a nation great; and the lesson thus taught must be of immense national service. Through the voice of the big, busy, practical, money-making city of Chicago America herself declares: Lo, it is not Mammon you should worship, but the light-bringing, health-giving gods of intelligence, refinement, and beauty! (*Week,* 78)

Reconsidering the legacy of the fair in the year of its centennial, Arnold Berke confirms that the White City, though it did not transform America, at least created "a collective memory—practically a consensus—of what our cities should look like."[20] This vision of the ideal city became, in turn, a catalyst for the City Beautiful movement, an attempt to bring such ideals to life through landscape architecture and urban planning. Today, says Berke, "as planners rediscover their roots, they are becoming reacquainted with the positive values of the City Beautiful approach—its accent on city structure, on urban beauty, on collaboration among the arts, and on that casualty of modern urban life, civic pride."

A hundred years ago, Frank Baum made the vision of the City Beautiful his own—and in so doing transmitted that ideal to generations of American children. Classic children's literature has sometimes been criticized for undervaluing the city; in stories like *The Wind in the Willows* and *Heidi,* the rural, natural setting is preferred over the urban, "artificial" one, despite the fact that most children live in cities and towns. In Oz, both the green countryside and the green city are wonderful places, where any child would love to be.

# 5

## Dorothy Opens the Door:
## The Inner Landscape of Oz

In the years following the Chicago Fair, Frank Baum began publishing his creative work. His first book, a collection of short tales called *Mother Goose in Prose* (1897), was based on stories he used to tell his younger sons, Kenneth and Harry, "explaining" the strange happenings in the Mother Goose rhymes. According to Baum family tradition, it was his formidable mother-in-law who first urged him to write the stories down and send them to a publisher. The book was accepted by the Chicago firm of Way and Williams and illustrated in black and white by a young artist named Maxfield Parrish, who had never illustrated a book before. Today both Baum and Parrish are avidly collected, and a single copy of *Mother Goose in Prose* in good condition would sell for several thousand dollars; at the time, it did moderately well—well enough, at least, to give Baum the encouragement he needed.

In 1899 Baum collaborated for the first time with the future illustrator of *The Wizard of Oz*, William Wallace Denslow. *Father Goose, His Book,* a volume of humorous verse full of colorful pictures, was an unexpected success—the best-selling children's book of the year. The profits paid for a summer cottage on Lake Macatawa in Michigan, which Baum called "The Sign of the Goose." Around 1896 he had completed a book of loosely connected fairy tales about a country called Phunnyland; this was finally published in 1900 under the title *A New Wonderland*—another indication that Baum saw Lewis Carroll as his predecessor.[1] But he had also undertaken a far more ambitious project—a full-length fantasy about a little girl who finds herself transported from Kansas to an imaginary world.

How Baum first came to write down the story and how Oz got its name are related in three separate accounts: *To Please a Child,* by Frank Joslyn Baum (his oldest son) and Russell P. MacFall; an interview given by Baum to the St. Louis *Republic* on 10 May 1903; and a letter he wrote to his publisher several years later. The Baum-MacFall version is unfortunately presented in semifictionalized form with reconstructed dialogue, making it impossible to tell how much is actual memory and how much surmise. In this version, Baum is telling the story to a group of children when a little girl named Tweety Robbins asks, " 'Oh, please, Mr. Baum! Where did the Scarecrow and the Tin Woodman live?' " (107). Baum scans the room and then tells the children that they lived in the Land of Oz. After the children have gone home, he confides to Maud that he found the name on an old two-drawer filing cabinet whose bottom drawer was labeled O-Z. " 'Right now,' " he says, " 'I am thinking of writing a long story about Dorothy and the Scarecrow; something like the story I was telling the children tonight' "(110). Later he remembers the date Oz was named because it was the same day—7 May 1898—that the news reached Chicago of Admiral Dewey's victory at Manila Bay. In 1899 he begins work on the new book, which he has decided to call *The Emerald City.*

> He wrote in longhand on letter size typewriter paper, using a soft, thick lead pencil. In the study of the home which he built more than a decade later in Hollywood hung a picture frame containing the stub of a pencil attached to a sheet of paper. On the paper is written: "With this pencil I wrote *The Emerald City.*" (111)

The explanation to Baum's publishers paints a slightly different picture:

> I was sitting ... in the hall, telling the kids a story and suddenly this one moved right in and took possession. I shooed the children away and grabbed a piece of paper that was lying there on the rack and began to write. It really seemed to write itself. Then I couldn't find any regular paper, so I took anything at all, even a bunch of old envelopes. (Hearn 1973, 27)

The St. Louis *Republic* interview gives the first published version of the filing cabinet anecdote:

> I have a little cabinet letter file on my desk in front of me. I was thinking and wondering about a title for my story, and I had settled on "Wizard" as part of it. My gaze was caught by the gilt letters on the three drawers of the cabinet. The first was A-G; the next drawer was labeled H-N; and on the last were the letters O-Z. And Oz it at once became. (Hearn 1973, 103)

While there is a kind of rough agreement between these accounts, there are also significant discrepancies. According to Baum and MacFall, the story is already well advanced when a direct question from Tweety Robbins inspires Baum to look at the filing cabinet; he does not begin writing the story until a year later, and his working title is *The Emerald City*. According to the explanation given his publishers, he begins writing the story down as soon as the idea occurs to him. And according to the interview, he happens to look at the filing cabinet while trying to think up a title for the story. Although we would normally expect an author to give the most authoritative account of his own creative process, we should keep in mind Baum's fondness for inventing a good yarn. A friend, Eunice Tietjens, wrote of him that "[e]verything he said had to be taken with at least a half-pound of salt. But he was a fascinating companion" (Gardner and Nye, 28). A nephew, Henry B. Brewster, remembered that "Mr. Baum always liked to tell wild tales, with a perfectly straight face, and earnestly, as though he really believed them himself" (43). Brewster described how Baum used to tease his devout mother by inventing quotations supposedly from the Bible; she always got out her Bible and searched for them, even though she had been fooled before. Baum's version of how Oz got its name is highly dramatic and nicely calculated to appeal to a reporter; indeed, he repeated this anecdote to other reporters on several occasions, and popular magazines and newspapers have not tired of it yet. Oz scholars, knowing Baum's fondness for tall tales, have been more skeptical.[2]

What Baum says about shooing the children out when the idea first grabbed him has an unsentimental ring of truth about it. This account, moreover, need not contradict the Baum and MacFall description of the evening story session; after beginning to write, he probably tried out the story on his young listeners. But did the writing begin in 1898 or 1899? Was it a question from Tweety Robbins that prompted him to invent the name Oz, or did it happen alone in his study? Did the filing cabinet with the O-Z drawer have two drawers or three—or did it even exist? In any case, Baum could not have been searching for a title for his new book the way he describes it in the interview. As Michael Patrick Hearn points out, " 'Oz' was part of at least two early titles for the book before 'wizard' was even considered" (1973, 103). Baum's first preference was for *The Emerald City,* as the evidence of the pencil indicates. When Baum was told of a publisher's superstition that no book with a jewel in the title could be successful, he suggested *From Kansas to Fairyland,* then *The Fairyland of Oz,* and then a shorter version, *The Land of Oz,* before finally choosing *The Wonderful Wizard of Oz.* The most likely origin of the name "Oz" is that Baum invented it as easily as he invented innumerable other strange names for the Oz books—and thought up the interesting explanation later. This has been confirmed by Maud Baum herself, who wrote in 1947, "The word Oz came out of Mr. Baum's mind, just as did his queer characters. No one or anything suggested the word— or any person. *This is a fact.*"[3]

The name "Dorothy," on the other hand, probably did have a special meaning for Baum, in this case one that he preferred to keep private. Baum and his family denied repeatedly that he chose the name for any personal reason. Yet it has been surmised for some time that Dorothy Gale of the Oz books was named after Dorothy Gage, Baum's niece, who died at the age of four months in 1898—the same period during which Baum first conceived the story of *The Wizard.*[4] Frank Joslyn Baum's insistence that "[a]t the time that he wrote *The*

*Wizard of Oz,* he did not know any girl or woman by the name of Dorothy" (Hearn 1973, 91) would have been literally true of Dorothy Gage. In 1996 the historian Sally Roesch Wagner discovered the actual tombstone of the dead child—the daughter of Maud's brother Thomas—in a cemetery in Bloomington, Indiana.[5] Earlier that year, Maud's mother had also died, and when Maud went to her niece's funeral, she was so overwhelmed with grief that she needed medical attention ("Real," 5). It seems impossible that Baum could have used the name Dorothy at this time without thinking of Dorothy Gage, and the similarity of the last names "Gage" and "Gale" supports this theory. Baum probably hoped to please and perhaps comfort Maud by giving this name to his appealing heroine. He and Maud had four sons, but they had always wanted a daughter, too.

Indeed, Baum's family relationships may have played a more significant role in the creation of *The Wizard of Oz* than is generally acknowledged. Few authors have been such devoted family men. Baum was so attached to Maud that during his years as a traveling salesman, he wrote to her every day. On one occasion when he did not hear from her and became alarmed, his disapproving mother-in-law called him "a perfect baby" (Carpenter and Shirley, 44). Every week, he gave Maud a box of candy. After his death, Maud wrote to her sister Helen, "He told me many times I was the only one he had ever loved.... For nearly thirty-seven years we had been everything to each other, we were happy, and now I am alone, to face the world alone" (123). The dedication of *The Wizard of Oz* to "my good friend and comrade / My Wife" was yet another expression of Baum's love for Maud. He was a loving father, too, who delighted in the company of his sons and hated to punish them; when, on one rare occasion, he spanked Kenneth, he later woke his son up to apologize (44).

The tales in *Mother Goose in Prose* had first been told as bedtime stories to Kenneth and Harry. Whichever account of *The Wizard's* writing is more accurate, there is general agreement that it, too, originated in stories Baum told to his sons. In 1898 Harry was nine and Kenneth seven—impressionable ages, and just right for fairy tales. As Baum's fantasy took form, whatever beyond pure enjoyment he wanted to convey was probably meant primarily for them.

## Dorothy Opens the Door

In his famous series of Babar books, the French children's author Jean de Brunhoff gave his own sons—and other children—a model of how one should construct one's life. In *The Story of Babar* (*Histoire de Babar,* 1931), the little elephant learns to wear clothes, gets an education, grows up, gets married, and is chosen King of the Elephants. But this is only the beginning of Babar's story; in subsequent volumes, he leads his people to a bloodless victory over the invading Rhinoceroses, builds a new capital for his kingdom and rules wisely over it, copes with depression and the serious illness of his beloved Old Lady, and raises three little elephants of his own. Babar, in other words, finds a way to introduce to young children the basic challenges of human life—growing up, marriage, war, sickness, finding a career, raising children—and the qualities one needs to meet those challenges successfully.

In *The Wizard of Oz,* Baum seems equally determined to provide guidance to his own and other children in their journey through life. Indeed, as with many authors before and after him, the journey is the metaphor he chooses; the physical journey of his protagonist through space represents the universal human passage through time. Like Babar, however, Dorothy is not merely an Everyman but a model for children to emulate—which seems particularly appropriate if Dorothy was conceived in part as a memorial to Dorothy Gage. She is sensible, friendly, helpful, brave without being foolhardy, deeply attached to her friends and family, and resolute in pursuing her goals. She does not change dramatically in the course of the journey, for this is not the story of someone who badly needs to change (like Bilbo in *The Hobbit* or Mary Lennox in *The Secret Garden*) but a story of self-discovery, in which Dorothy comes to realize her own potential by journey's end. In this interpretation, the Scarecrow, the Tin Woodman, and the Cowardly Lion represent not only the friends we all need to help us on our way but also the qualities Baum felt were most essential for the traveler—qualities that Dorothy is to find within herself.

As the story opens, Dorothy is shown in contrast to her bleak environment and her unsmiling aunt and uncle: "When Dorothy, who was an orphan, first came to her, Aunt Em had been so startled by the child's laughter that she would scream and press her hand upon her heart whenever Dorothy's merry laugh reached her ears; and she still looked at the little girl with wonder that she could find anything to laugh at" (*Wizard*, 8). Like many of the classic children's authors, Baum had assimilated the Romantic view of childhood as a naturally innocent and joyous time of life. Children, the Romantics believed, were closer to nature than adults, and Dorothy's innocent joy is preserved by her close relationship with an animal—her dog, Toto. "It was Toto that made Dorothy laugh and saved her from growing as gray as her other surroundings.... Toto played all day long, and Dorothy played with him, and loved him dearly" (8). Dorothy, at this point, seems unconscious of anything beyond her own enjoyment; she laughs, she plays, and she loves her dog—more clearly than she loves her unresponsive aunt and uncle, let alone her dead parents (who are never mentioned). The dog's name may be significant; the Latin *totus* means "all," and Toto is everything to Dorothy. Her love for Toto delays her escape from the cyclone, for she is determined not to leave him behind.

Not until Dorothy is caught up by the cyclone does Baum move us closer to her point of view and give us a sense of her inner strength. Tears, screams, fainting, even panic would be understandable; it is impressive that Dorothy gives way to none of these. Though Toto runs frantically, barking, around the room, "Dorothy sat quite still on the floor and waited to see what would happen" (9). When the dog falls through the open trap-door, she pulls him up again, "afterward closing the trap-door so that no more accidents could happen.... At first she had wondered if she would be dashed to pieces when the house fell again; but as the hours passed and nothing terrible happened, she stopped worrying and resolved to wait calmly and see what the future would bring" (10). Dorothy's self-command and presence of mind show the reader what kind of person she is even before she gets to Oz—and give children a useful model of how to behave in a frightening situation.

In Oz, Baum sees to it that Dorothy must rely almost entirely on her own resources. She tries to get help from the first adults she meets—the Good Witch of the North and the Munchkins who accompany her—but they can do nothing for her; they have never even heard of Kansas, and their own world, they tell her, is surrounded by an impassable desert. When the Good Witch says that Dorothy must go to the City of Emeralds and seek the Wizard's aid, Dorothy pleads, " 'Won't you go with me?' "—for she has "begun to look upon the little old woman as her only friend." The Witch replies simply, " 'No, I cannot do that' "(17). Her only gift to Dorothy is a protective kiss on her forehead, but Dorothy seems largely unaware of the power of the kiss; perhaps it represents something like the child's own innocent goodness, which would lose its power if the child consciously exploited it.

Fortunately, Dorothy proves herself capable of a high degree of independence. Her good sense enables her to adapt quickly to what is unfamiliar; for example, it is her own idea to wear the Silver Shoes on her journey, reasoning that " '[t]hey would be just the thing to take a long walk in, for they could not wear out' "(18). She knows how to take care of herself, too. Left alone, she finds fruit and water for her lunch, washes herself and puts on a clean dress, and prepares a basket of food to take with her on her journey; she even remembers to lock the door behind her when she sets off for the city she has never heard of before. And once on her way—having found the yellow brick road herself—she enjoys her new surroundings: "The sun shone bright and the birds sang sweet and Dorothy did not feel nearly as bad as you might think a little girl would who had been suddenly whisked away from her own country and set down in the midst of a strange land" (18). She spends a pleasant evening celebrating the death of the Wicked Witch of the East with some Munchkins and stays the night at their house. The next morning, though warned that " 'you must pass through rough and dangerous places before you reach the end of your journey,' " Dorothy "bravely resolved not to turn back" (21). That day she spies the Scarecrow stuck on his pole and kindly rescues him.

The characters of the Scarecrow, the Tin Woodman, and the Cowardly Lion are so memorable and the image of all four travelers together on the yellow brick road so strong—in large part, thanks to the MGM movie—that it is easy to overlook Dorothy's independence and competence in these first chapters. For children just setting out on their own journeys into a strange new world, however, Baum's implicit suggestion that they will be able to survive and flourish like Dorothy is reassuring and encouraging. It must have been especially satisfying for the girls of a century ago—perhaps for Maud Baum, too—to see a little girl managing so well on her own.

In chapters 3 through 6, Dorothy is joined by her three companions, each hoping that the great Wizard will give him what he needs most. The Scarecrow yearns for brains, the Tin Woodman for a loving heart, and the Cowardly Lion for courage. Though the characters argue over which of these qualities is most important, the argument is never won, and it seems clear that all three are essential. In fact, though Baum does not state this explicitly, all the dangers and difficulties that the travelers encounter on their way to the Emerald City— from the great ditches across the road and the battle with the Kalidahs (chapter 7) to the river crossing and the Deadly Poppy Field (chapter 8)—require that they work together and combine their separate abilities to overcome these obstacles. Baum also leaves it to the young reader to discover that these three characters already possess to a marked degree the qualities they seek. Although the Scarecrow seems comic and foolish at first—always falling into holes because he does not know enough to walk around them (24)—it is he who finds food for Dorothy, figures out how to get across the ditches and how to kill the Kalidahs, and suggests that the Tin Woodman build them a raft to cross the river. The Tin Woodman's tenderheartedness is revealed when he steps on a beetle by accident and kills it: "This made the Tin Woodman very unhappy, for he was always careful not to hurt any living creature; and as he walked along he wept several tears of sorrow and regret" (39). "The Tin Woodman knew very well he had no heart," Baum explains, "and therefore he took great care never to be cruel or unkind to anything" (40)—inviting young readers to puzzle over this paradox. The Cowardly Lion, "although he was certainly afraid" (43), prepares to fight the Kalidahs to the death. When the humbug Wizard finally rewards the three, to their satisfaction, with visible symbols of intelligence, love, and courage, even a small child can understand that the only difference this makes is in their imaginations.

Again, one might not notice that Dorothy herself possesses the three essential qualities. Her ability to adapt to unfamiliar conditions is good evidence of her intelligence. Her love for Toto is clear when she risks death to save him from the cyclone and the Lion, and her rescue of the Scarecrow shows that she is kind even to strangers. Her willingness to brave, alone, the unknown dangers of her journey shows that she has courage, too.

Reaching the Emerald City, of course, does not solve Dorothy's problem of how to return to Kansas; indeed, the second section of the book, in which she must conquer the Wicked Witch of the West, is a greater test of her inner resources than the first. As Dorothy, sobbing, protests to the Wizard, " 'I never killed anything, willingly, ... and even if I want to, how could I kill the Wicked Witch?' "(68). She faces a moral dilemma as well as an enemy more powerful than the Wizard himself, and it is the moral aspect that seems to trouble her most. When the Lion (appropriately) proposes that the four of them " 'seek out the Wicked Witch, and destroy her,' " Dorothy concludes, " 'I suppose we must try it; but I am sure I do not want to kill anybody, even to see Aunt Em again' "(72). Baum has created a situation in which one of Dorothy's essential qualities—her kind and loving heart—conflicts directly with the task she has been assigned. He refuses, moreover—unlike many filmmakers today—to resolve the dilemma by having Dorothy realize that in a dangerous world, she must overcome her scruples and become a killer, too. Dorothy must somehow retain her kindness and defeat the Witch as well.

Though less dominant in the book than in the MGM film version, the Witch is by far the most frightening danger Dorothy faces; if any section of *The Wizard* gives a child the "heart-aches and nightmares" that Baum insisted he had left out, it will probably be this one. When the four friends easily overcome the four armies that the Witch sends against them—once again, by combining their separate abilities—a reassuring pattern is created, which makes their overwhelming defeat by the Winged Monkeys all the more appalling. And although Dorothy is unharmed (being protected by the Good Witch's kiss), it is horrifying for a tenderhearted young reader to see the Tin Woodman hurled from a great height onto the rocks and the Scarecrow ruthlessly dismantled. As James Thurber testifies, "I know that I went through excruciatingly lovely nightmares and heartaches when the Scarecrow lost his straw, when the Tin Woodman was taken apart, when the Saw-Horse broke his wooden leg (it hurt for me even if it didn't for Mr. Baum)" (Hearn 1983, 160). Dorothy, moreover, does not understand that she is safe from physical harm. As the Winged Monkeys attack, she stands by stoically, "with Toto in her arms, watching the sad fate of her comrades and thinking it would soon be her turn" (*Wizard*, 79). When she is enslaved, she is "glad the Wicked Witch had decided not to kill her" (81) but remains "full of fear for herself and Toto" (82).

Baum clearly indicates at this point that Dorothy has the potential, if she can realize it, to free herself and conquer the Witch. The Witch is "surprised and worried" when she sees the protective mark on Dorothy's forehead and trembles with fear when she sees the Silver Shoes (79).

> At first the Witch was tempted to run away from Dorothy; but she happened to look into the child's eyes and saw how simple the soul behind them was, and that the little girl did not know of the wonderful power the Silver Shoes gave her. So the Wicked Witch laughed to herself, and thought, "I can still make her my slave, for she does not know how to use her power." (79–81)

However, Dorothy values the shoes enough to guard them carefully, and when the Witch finally succeeds in stealing one from her, Dorothy momentarily forgets her fear. She calls the Witch " 'a wicked creature!' " to her face and demands her shoe; when the Witch, laughing, promises to get the other shoe as well, "this made Dorothy so very angry that she picked up the bucket of water that stood near and dashed it over the Witch, wetting her from head to foot." The next moment she sees the Witch—in Baum's vivid and homely simile— "melting away like brown sugar before her very eyes" (83).

Dorothy's ignorance of the traditional aversion witches have for water ingeniously allows her to destroy her enemy and yet retain her innocence. The MGM film pressed this point more insistently; in that version, Dorothy throws the bucket of water over the Scarecrow to save him from burning and splashes the Witch by mistake. In Baum's story, Dorothy's attack on the Witch is no meaningless accident. She seems to realize instinctively that the Witch's theft of her shoes will rob her of something essential to herself, and her sense of outrage is stronger than her fear of the Witch. Once again, Baum encourages the child's desire for independence, first by isolating Dorothy from outside aid and then—even more radically—by creating circumstances in which disobedience, anger, and open defiance of an authority figure become the key to freedom.

Dorothy's actions after she has destroyed the Witch, moreover, display more power than she has ever shown before. Although she is frightened to see the Witch melting, and even apologizes to her, she treats the oozing brown remains with calm practicality and no sense of squeamishness:

> Seeing that she had really melted away to nothing, Dorothy drew another bucket of water and threw it over the mess. She then swept it all out the door. After picking out the silver shoe, which was all that was left of the old woman, she cleaned and dried it with a cloth, and put it on her foot again. Then, being at last free to do as she chose, she ran out to the court-yard to tell the Lion that the Wicked Witch of the West had come to an end, and that they were no longer prisoners in a strange land. (83–84)

After freeing the Lion from his cage, Dorothy takes charge in the Witch's Castle: "Dorothy's first act was to call all the Winkies together and tell them that they were no longer slaves" (84). It is she who personally directs the grateful Winkies in rescuing and restoring the Woodman and the Scarecrow. Upon leaving the Witch's Castle, she takes with her the Golden Cap—yet another source of power, which, like the Silver Shoes, "fitted her exactly" (88). When the four companions get lost on their way back to the Emerald City, Dorothy thinks of calling the Field Mice to their aid and thus learns that through the Cap she now has command of the Flying Monkeys. Dorothy has not only retained her own power but gained much of the Witch's power as well, and she makes conscious use of it when she orders the no longer frightening Monkeys to carry her and her companions to the City.

Yet she still expects a powerful adult to solve her biggest problem. As long as she retains the illusion that the Wizard can get her

Dorothy supervises as the Winkies repair the Tin Woodman.
*Original illustration by W. W. Denslow for* The Wonderful Wizard of Oz
*(Chicago: George M. Hill, 1900).*

back to Kansas, she remains unable to realize her full potential and solve the problem herself. Although Baum's disappointment with the politicians of his day may have helped shape his conception of the Wizard, the revelation that the Wizard has no magical powers also implies that the adults who seem so powerful to children are no more than human beings: " 'I'm really a very good man,' " the Wizard tells Dorothy, " 'but I'm a very bad Wizard, I must admit' "(100). And while the Wizard does his human best to help Dorothy, his solution—the balloon—works only for himself, not for her.

After the Wizard leaves her behind, Dorothy asks the Winged Monkeys to carry her across the desert to Kansas, but these magical creatures cannot leave their own world for one in which they don't exist. The kindly soldier with the green whiskers, however, suggests that Glinda, the Good Witch of the South, may know what to do; so Dorothy and her three companions set out once more, traveling through the wood of the fighting trees, the China Country, the forest of the spider monster, and over the hill of the Hammer-Heads to reach the Quadling Country, where Glinda reigns.

This final section of *The Wizard* has been much criticized as "anticlimactic" by C. Warren Hollister and others, and the MGM movie omits it altogether. In the latter version, after the Wizard has taken off, Glinda at once descends in her bubble into the Emerald City Square and instructs Dorothy to tap her heels together, while repeating to herself, "There's no place like home." Baum nonetheless has his reasons for including the journey to the Quadling Country. Rather than waiting passively for another powerful adult to appear—*dea ex machina*—and tell her what to do, Baum's Dorothy must exert herself and face new perils to earn Glinda's aid. She has three companions who embody three essential qualities, and in Baum's scheme she makes three journeys, too, traveling each time through a different part of Oz. Certain features of this third journey, moreover, relate it more closely than either of the first two to Dorothy's desire to return home.

Kansas is, of course, a far less attractive place than Oz, as Baum is perfectly aware. At the very outset of Dorothy's acquaintance with the Scarecrow, she tells him "all about Kansas and how gray everything was there."

The Scarecrow listened carefully, and said,

"I cannot understand why you should wish to leave this beautiful country and go back to the dry, gray place you call Kansas."

"That is because you have no brains," answered the girl. "No matter how dreary and gray our homes are, we people of flesh and blood would rather live there than in any other country, be it ever so beautiful. There is no place like home."

The Scarecrow sighed.

"Of course I cannot understand it," he said. "If your heads were stuffed with straw, like mine, you would probably all live in the beautiful places, and then Kansas would have no people at all. It is fortunate for Kansas that you have brains." (25)

Unable to refute this, Dorothy changes the subject. One of the principal changes made by the MGM screenwriters was to take her argument at face value and amplify it into the main theme of the movie—in the book, this is the only time she says, "There is no place like home"—while ignoring the Scarecrow's trenchant reply. To a reader capable of perceiving irony, however, it's obvious that Baum (as one might expect from his life story) felt no sentimental attachment to the midwestern farm country. Indeed, having spent several summers at the Hotel del Coronado in San Diego, California, he and Maud moved from Chicago to Hollywood in 1910, where they built a house called Ozcot. Southern California was beautiful in those days before smog and freeways, warm and sunny and full of flowers—perhaps as close as one could come to Oz. Baum had only one reason to think fondly of Aberdeen: it was the town where two of his sons were born and where he and Maud began to raise their family. And love of her family is the only thing that ties Dorothy to Kansas, too.

At the beginning of *The Wizard*, as we have seen, the carefree Dorothy shows little evidence of loving her aunt and uncle, but leaving home—in this interpretation, beginning to grow up—seems to awaken a new and thoughtful affection for them. " 'I am anxious to get back to my Aunt and Uncle, for I am sure they will worry about me' "(16), she tells the Good Witch of the North. In the Emerald City, she dreams that she is back in Kansas, "where Aunt Em was telling her how glad she was to have her little girl at home again" (95). In her dream, Aunt Em seems more motherly than at the outset of the story; perhaps it is because Dorothy now realizes that Aunt Em is all the mother she will ever have. Her final interview with Glinda shows a fully mature awareness and concern for her relatives' financial difficulties:

> "My greatest wish now ... is to get back to Kansas, for Aunt Em will surely think something dreadful has happened to me, and that will make her put on mourning; and unless the crops are better this year than they were last I am sure Uncle Henry cannot afford it."
>
> Glinda leaned forward and kissed the sweet, upturned face of the loving little girl.
>
> "Bless your dear heart," she said, "I am sure I can tell you of a way to get back to Kansas." (128–30)

Baum's adjectives "sweet" and "loving," and Glinda's blessing reinforce the point that Dorothy's unaccountable desire to return to Kansas is motivated by love alone. And Glinda herself, an appealing mother figure, represents what Dorothy yearns to find waiting for her.

In this final section of the story, Baum emphasizes the key role of love through Dorothy's three companions as well. In the first and second sections, their quest was to achieve their own separate goals; they accompany Dorothy on the third journey simply because they care about her. Even the Scarecrow, who has just become ruler of the Emerald City, abandons his new throne, declaring gratefully that " 'my good luck is all due to her, and I shall never leave her until she starts back to Kansas for good and all' "(113). When Dorothy finally says good-bye to the three, she hugs and kisses them and finds herself crying "at this sorrowful parting from her loving comrades" (132). Glinda's generous kindness in this scene, not only to Dorothy but to the Winged Monkeys—whom she promises to set free forever, once they have carried the three companions home again—further heightens the sense of love as a motivating force. Even the red fences and houses of Glinda's Quadling Country, the "handsome red uniforms" of her girl guards, and the "rich red" (128) of her hair repeat the warm color traditionally associated with love. Baum's illustrator,

Dorothy gives Glinda the Golden Cap.
*Original illustration by W. W. Denslow for* The Wonderful Wizard of Oz
*(Chicago: George M. Hill, 1900).*

William Denslow, made the association even more explicit by decorating Glinda's crown and dress, as well as the uniforms of her guards, with red hearts.

All this provides the context for the short but wholly satisfying final chapter, in which Aunt Em—the same aunt who could hardly bear to hear her laugh—greets the returning Dorothy with an outpouring of motherly affection, just as in her dream. " 'My darling child!' she cried, folding the little girl in her arms and covering her face with kisses; 'where in the world did you come from?' "(132). Perhaps Dorothy's disappearance has simply made Aunt Em realize how much she loves her; but it also seems as if Dorothy's awareness that she loves and needs her aunt—an awareness that she had to leave home to find—has awakened a loving response in Aunt Em as well. Perhaps for Baum, on the most personal level, it meant that the lost Dorothy might not be lost forever—that there might be a loving reunion someday with the child who was mourned as dead.

Yet neither Glinda's magic nor Dorothy's love is what transports her back to Kansas. She must call upon the power within herself to achieve her heart's desire—a power she has had all along but been unconscious of, and which is given concrete form in the Silver Shoes. " 'Your Silver Shoes will carry you over the desert,' " Glinda tells her. " 'If you had known their power you could have gone back to your Aunt Em the very first day you came to this country' "(131). Her three friends point out, however, that had Dorothy done so, they would never have fulfilled their own potential; as the Tin Woodman puts it, " 'I might have stood and rusted in the forest till the end of the world.' " Now each rules in his own kingdom—the Scarecrow in the Emerald City, the Woodman in the Winkie Country, and the Lion in the forest. You are born, Baum suggests, with the power to achieve your heart's desire, but only your journey through life can develop your intelligence, your courage, and your ability to give love.

Throughout the story, Baum consistently depicts Dorothy as a source of power, not only by making her brave and capable and successful, but through her relationships with the other characters. Dorothy's three companions, though aware that she is physically weaker than they are, all regard her as their equal (and, in two cases, their rescuer). She is Toto's protector throughout the story. The Munchkins and other Oz folk, described as child-size—"about as tall as Dorothy" (12)—treat her more like an adult than a little girl. The only genuinely "adult" characters—those with real authority and power—are the four Witches and the Wizard. In Baum's world, being a Witch or Wizard has nothing to do with worshiping or allying oneself with the Devil; it simply means that one has mastered magic—the greatest source of power in a "fairyland" like Oz. The Munchkins believe that Dorothy must be a Witch herself, since she has killed the Wicked Witch of the East. Indeed, Dorothy displays a power greater than that of both Wicked Witches, whom she kills single-handedly, while she and her friends expose the false power of the Wizard.

To translate this into the terms of child psychology, the Wizard is a rather feeble father figure who puts on a frightening show of authority, while the four Witches are a composite mother figure. The splitting of the Witches into Good and Wicked follows the familiar pattern of the folktale, in which the nurturing and supportive aspects of the mother and her negative or destructive aspects are split into good and evil characters—often a mother and a stepmother. It makes sense that Dorothy, a female protagonist, would have more "mothers" than "fathers" to deal with, for it is through her mother that a girl comes to know the woman in herself. This type of folktale-related analysis seems particularly appropriate for the second section of *The Wizard,* for Baum was clearly influenced by "Hansel and Gretel" when he created the Wicked Witch of the West. Like Hansel and Gretel, Dorothy and the Lion become prisoners of the Witch, who keeps the Lion (like Hansel) in a cage and forces Dorothy (like Gretel) to do her housework. Dorothy (again like Gretel) manages to destroy the Witch and free them both.

Charles Perrault's "Cinderella," the story of a girl growing up, seems to have influenced Baum as well. Cinderella's stepmother (the bad mother) keeps her at home doing housework and tries to prevent her from using the power of her magic shoes to win her freedom; her father (like the Wizard) is good-natured but powerless to help his daughter; and her godmother (the good mother) gives Cinderella the shoes and the chance to use them—just as the Good Witch of the

North gives Dorothy the Silver Shoes, and Glinda teaches her how they work. This interpretation suggests that Dorothy finds her female identity a source of great power but that the power itself is morally neutral; the Silver Shoes can be used by anyone who wears them. (The same principle holds true for the more limited power of the Golden Cap; we see the same Winged Monkeys used to commit cruel and destructive acts by the Wicked Witch of the West and helpful acts by Dorothy and Glinda.) Again Dorothy provides a positive model; when she consciously unleashes her full power at last, she does so for the sake of those she loves.[6]

In 1900, when *The Wizard of Oz* was published, Frank Baum was 44—old enough to look back on his own life's journey and sum up what he had learned from it. If *The Wizard* itself can be taken as evidence, he realized that both intelligence and courage had helped him through the repeated failures of his early years to the success of his window-decorating enterprises and his new career as a writer, but that love for his wife and sons had given him the motivation to keep trying until he succeeded, as well as the happiness that was his chief reward. Like Dorothy, he had been forced into independence—in his case, by his father's death and the failure of the family business—and had discovered within himself a strength that he had probably never suspected he possessed. C. S. Lewis declared in his famous essay "On Three Ways of Writing for Children" that "[t]he only moral that is of any value is that which arises inevitably from the whole cast of the author's mind."[7] This seems to have been the case with *The Wizard of Oz;* whatever Baum had to say was based not on any theory of what children should learn but on his personal experience and his own deeply held convictions.

Fantasy offered Baum a way of expressing his beliefs with greater clarity than could be afforded by mimetic fiction; no realistic human character, for example, could claim literally not to have a brain and go in search of one. But his characters and their actions were not his only resources. Because *The Wizard* takes place largely in an imaginary world, the world itself could be designed to help express Baum's concepts and ideas.

Dorothy—and with her, the reader—learns the general topography of Oz only moments after her arrival, when the Munchkins and the Good Witch of the North explain why they cannot help her return to Kansas:

> "At the East, not far from here," said one, "there is a great desert, and none could live to cross it."
>
> "It is the same at the South," said another, "for I have been there and seen it. The South is the country of the Quadlings."
>
> "I am told," said the third man, "that it is the same at the West. And that country, where the Winkies live, is ruled by the wicked Witch of the West, who would make you her slave if you passed her way."
>
> "The North is my home," said the old lady, "and at its edge is the same great desert that surrounds this land of Oz. I'm afraid, my dear, you will have to live with us." (16)

The Good Witch also informs Dorothy that the Emerald City " 'is exactly in the center of the country.' " Thus, from the outset, we know that Oz is divided compasswise into four main countries, with the Emerald City at the center, like the hub of a wheel, and the desert surrounding the whole of it, like the rim. We also gradually become aware that each country is associated with a different color. The Munchkins of the East wear blue and live in blue houses, the Winkies yellow, and the Quadlings red, while in the Emerald City everything is green. (Baum does not reveal in *The Wizard* that the North is the Gillikin Country, whose prevailing color is purple.) As for the yellow brick road, Michael Patrick Hearn asks, "What would be more logical than a yellow brick road to travel on through a blue countryside en route to a green city?" (1973, 107).

The basic topography of Oz thus corresponds to the five characters who represent power and authority—the four female Witches (symmetrically positioned, with the two Good Witches to the North and South and the two Wicked Witches to the East and West) and the one male Wizard in the middle. When Baum's critics object to Dorothy's journey to the South, they might well ask not why Baum adds an "anticlimactic" third journey but why Dorothy does not visit all four regions of Oz. It seems that in this instance Baum was more concerned with his theme of the three essential qualities, to which

Dorothy's journeys correspond, than with the quadrilateral symmetry of his world.

Baum also designed his imaginary world in a way that reinforces the metaphor of the journey through life. In this respect, he may have been influenced by John Bunyan's classic journey allegory *The Pilgrim's Progress,* as J. Karl Franson claims, for like Bunyan he creates a route full of obstacles; some are natural features, like the ravines, the broad river, and the Poppy Field, some local monsters like the Kalidahs and the Hammer-Heads. The yellow brick road clearly indicates the path one must follow through life to reach one's goal, but Baum never suggests that the path is an easy one. In the second section of the story, which presents even greater challenges to Dorothy and her friends than the first, there is no path at all.

> "Which road leads to the Wicked Witch of the West?" asked Dorothy.
> "There is no road," answered the Guardian of the Gates; "no one ever wishes to go that way." (*Wizard,* 74)

Baum's most powerful use of setting as conceptual tool, however, is the contrast between Kansas and Oz. In their discussion of the imaginary worlds of science fiction, Robert Holdstock and Malcolm Edwards suggest that some of these worlds function "as objective correlatives, giving physical expression to ideas or psychological states."[8] Baum's Kansas, though based on the actuality of the drought years he had witnessed in the Midwest, is also an objective correlative for depression and deprivation. The same gray that colors the plowed land and the dry grass permeates the souls of the joyless farming couple who live there. Only Toto, seemingly unaffected, saves Dorothy, too, "from growing as gray as her other surroundings" (8).

Their farmhouse, though once painted, is now "as dull and gray as everything else" (8), and Baum pictures it in some detail, even before he describes the land and the people—foreshadowing the pivotal role it will play in the story:

> Their house was small, for the lumber to build it had to be carried by wagon many miles. There were four walls, a floor and a roof,

> which made one room; and this room contained a rusty looking cooking stove, a cupboard for the dishes, a table, three or four chairs, and the beds. Uncle Henry and Aunt Em had a big bed in one corner, and Dorothy a little bed in another corner. There was no garret at all, and no cellar—except a small hole, dug in the ground, called a cyclone cellar, where the family could go in case one of those great whirlwinds arose, mighty enough to crush any building in its path. It was reached by a trap-door in the middle of the floor, from which a ladder led down into the small, dark hole. (7–8)

This is no cozy pioneer home like those in the Little House books but a place of grim poverty, constantly threatened by destruction.

In *The Poetics of Space,* the psychologist Gaston Bachelard maintains that the image of the house represents "the topography of our intimate being."[9] He gives the example of Henri Bosco's *Malicroix,* in which a little house—"a humble house" that "appears to lack resistance" (43)—bravely withstands the fury of a storm, becoming a symbol both of maternal protection for the man it shelters and of human virtue in a harsh and hostile world. The drawings of houses made by children, Bachelard points out, are used by child psychologists as an aid to understanding their state of well-being. He quotes Anne Balif: " 'Asking a child to draw his house is asking him to reveal the deepest dream shelter he has found for his happiness. If he is happy, he will succeed in drawing a snug, protected house which is well built on deeply-rooted foundations' "(72). Bachelard adds, "If the child is unhappy, however, the house bears traces of his distress."

If we consider Dorothy's house in Kansas as a key to her psyche, it tells us that Dorothy is unhappy, and even suggests why. The barely furnished, unprotected house, not built on "deeply-rooted foundations" but perched over a cyclone cellar, is a place without warmth, comfort, or security. However carefree she may appear to be, Dorothy is an orphan; she has lost the love and security of her parents and is living with an aunt and uncle too locked up in their own unhappiness to show much affection for her. The ominous description of the cyclone cellar under the house, with its trapdoor in the floor and "small, dark hole"—an apt image of death and the grave—suggests that she knows what has happened to her parents and is afraid that she, too, may have to go down the dark hole. Unlike the maternal house in *Malicroix,* Dorothy's house does not withstand the storm but is uprooted, just as Dorothy herself has been, and swept helplessly away into the unknown. Baum, we remember, wished to avoid heartaches and nightmares for his young audience; by displacing Dorothy's insecurity, unhappiness, and fear of death onto the house she inhabits, he can make them part of the story without disturbing the reader. As long as Dorothy remains calm, the reader will feel no more than pleasurable suspense, even in the midst of the cyclone.

The threat of death associated with the house is fulfilled—but again, it is not Dorothy who dies but someone the reader never actually sees and is not supposed to feel sorry for. It is also possible that when Dorothy's house—that is, the unhappy Dorothy—kills the "bad mother," she is unconsciously punishing the dead mother who deserted her. Whether or not Baum had this in mind, he is careful to exonerate Dorothy from consciously intending harm.

For everyone who sees the movie of *The Wizard,* the crux of the whole story is the moment when Dorothy opens the door. Commenting on the symbolism of doors, Bachelard remarks, "If one were to give an account of all the doors one has closed and opened, of all the doors one would like to re-open, one would have to tell the story of one's entire life" (224). Outside this door is a world of new possibilities, and Dorothy's readiness to enter the new world is a sign that she is ready to move forward in her life. She does not cling to her old, unhappy self; when she sets off for the Emerald City, she closes and locks the door behind her, and the bleak, gray house is never mentioned again.[10]

Her first glimpse of Oz is enough to tell her that she is no longer in Kansas:

> The cyclone had set the house down, very gently—for a cyclone—in the midst of a country of marvelous beauty. There were lovely patches of green sward all about, with stately trees bearing rich and luscious fruits. Banks of gorgeous flowers were on every hand, and birds with rare and brilliant plumage sang and fluttered in the trees and bushes. A little way off was a small brook, rushing and sparkling along between green banks, and

> murmuring in a voice very grateful to a little girl who had lived so
> long on the dry, gray prairies. (*Wizard*, 10–12)

Kansas was dry and gray and lifeless; Oz has a running brook, green lawns, trees, birds, and flowers. Kansas was a place of sensory deprivation; for Oz, in one short paragraph, Baum evokes the senses of sight, sound (singing birds and murmuring brook), smell (flowers), and taste ("rich and luscious fruits"). If the landscape of Kansas is an objective correlative for depression and emotional barrenness, the fertile landscape of Oz, which recalls the archetype of the paradisal garden, promises happiness and fulfillment. At the same time, Oz is not simply the opposite of Kansas but its transformation. Dorothy does not find herself on a seacoast or in the mountains but in prosperous farming country, such as Uncle Henry might have envisioned in his dreams. It is no wonder that she adjusts so easily to this world. Viewed as inner landscape, the countryside of Oz represents what Dorothy is free to discover within herself, once she leaves her unhappy, insecure old self behind. Not all of it will be beautiful, and some will be dangerous—self-discovery involves more than a stroll through pretty scenery.

Baum's use of contrasting settings extends to interior environments as well. Although Dorothy does not (on this trip) find a permanent home in Oz, the comfortless interior of the Kansas farmhouse can be compared with some of the rooms that provide her resting places during her journey. Her first night in Oz, for example, is spent in a Munchkin farmhouse, where she is the guest of honor at a party:

> When she had tired watching the dancing, Boq led her into the
> house, where he gave her a room with a pretty bed in it. The
> sheets were made of blue cloth, and Dorothy slept soundly in
> them till morning, with Toto curled up on the blue rug beside her.
> (21)

Brief though this description is, the room is obviously nicer than what she is used to; in Kansas, she did not even have a room of her own, but only a corner of the one-room house. Baum saves his best effort, however, for the Emerald City, where Dorothy is given a child's daydream of a bedroom:

It was the sweetest little room in the world, with a soft, comfortable bed that had sheets of green silk and a green velvet counterpane. There was a tiny fountain in the middle of the room, that shot a spray of green perfume into the air, to fall back into a beautifully carved green marble basin. Beautiful green flowers stood in the windows, and there was a shelf with a row of little green books. When Dorothy had time to open these books she found them full of queer green pictures that made her laugh, they were so funny.

In a wardrobe were many green dresses, made of silk and satin and velvet; and all of them fitted Dorothy exactly. (64)

The dresses that fit Dorothy "exactly" tell us that the room is not simply a guest room; in some magical way, it belongs to her. In terms of inner landscape, it represents the new self she has discovered in Oz. Later in the series, when Dorothy comes to Oz to stay, this room will be hers for good.

Although Baum's use of "inner landscape" in *The Wizard of Oz* fits Dorothy's situation so well, its appeal is universal. We all wish, at times, that our gray world—or our drab selves—could be magically transformed. Dorothy's journey also expresses universal themes, especially for children, who are just beginning their journeys through life and their discoveries of the potential within themselves. But Baum told this story only once; in the later Oz books, Oz becomes an end in itself. The following chapter suggests why generations of children have found this imaginary world so fascinating and satisfying.

# 6

# "Now We Can Cross the Shifting Sands":
# The Outer Landscape of Oz

The long-controversial status of the Oz books had at least one positive outcome. Because so many articulate adults have felt compelled to
defend their childhood favorites from the attacks of critics and librarians, we have more evidence on what these books meant to them than
in the case of most children's classics. A point that emerges—perhaps
unexpectedly—is that although *The Wizard of Oz* is by far the most
famous of the series and considered by many critics the only one
worth mentioning, it is by no means everyone's favorite. On the con-
trary, there is little consensus among those who loved the books as
children. James Thurber declares, "The first two, *The Wizard* and *The
Land,* are far and away the best" (Hearn 1983, 161). Gore Vidal, on
the other hand, writes that "as a child, I preferred *The Emerald City,
Rinkitink,* and *The Lost Princess* to *The Wizard.* Now I find that all of
the books tend to flow together in a single narrative, with occasional
bad patches" (257). Addressing fellow fans in *The Oz Gazette,* 12-
year-old Katy Lau mentions *Ozma of Oz* and a non-Baum Oz book,
*Queen Ann of Oz* by Eric Gjovaag and Karyl Carlson.[1] Fourteen-year-
old Ingrid Johnson tells me that her favorites were *The Land of Oz,*

*Ozma of Oz,* and *The Patchwork Girl of Oz.*[2] My own favorites were *The Emerald City* and *The Lost Princess.* Clearly there is enough variety within the series to satisfy individual tastes.

This wide range of favorites also suggests that the common element in children's enjoyment of the Oz books is neither a particular story line nor a particular character, but Oz itself. As Katy Lau puts it, "For me the lure of Oz is that it's a whole world inside books and it seems so real! . . . When I read the Oz books it's very easy to get lost in its magnificent world!" (8). She is echoed by 16-year-old Sarah Hayes: "Through the Oz books, one can escape from reality into a fantasy world. When I was little I used to dream about living in the Emerald City with Ozma, Dorothy, Betsy, and Trot."[3] As C. Warren Hollister declared, "Where is the theme? The theme is Oz" (Hearn 1983, 196).

That the series was continued after Baum's death by Ruth Plumly Thompson and others has been criticized as blatant commercial exploitation, but it is also striking evidence that the world of Oz had taken on a life of its own. The International Wizard of Oz Club, which welcomes fans, scholars, and collectors of all ages, not only allows the Oz books of Thompson and her successors into its canon but encourages its members to write original Oz stories. Their *Baum Bugle* (since 1957) includes articles on such subjects as Oz history, laws governing the use of magic in Oz, food in Oz, whether money exists in Oz, and the putative deadliness of the Deadly Desert. Minor inconsistencies in Baum's world are theorized and argued over with the same delight that the Baker Street Irregulars find in the inconsistencies of Sherlock Holmes.[4]

How did Baum manage to create a world with so high a degree of what Hollister calls "three-dimensionality" that it could outlast its own Royal Historian and still be alive and growing a hundred years after Dorothy first opened the door? What were the principles on which he constructed it, and how do these principles contribute to its continuing appeal? This chapter will explore these questions of what we may call the "outer landscape" of Oz—that is, the physical world of Oz as mental or conceptual construct, as opposed to the "inner landscape" or psychological construct analyzed in chapter 5.

Some of the writing techniques employed by Baum in *The Wizard of Oz* to create his world have been used by the creators of imaginary lands from Homer onward—techniques that include the use of detail, particularly sensory and concrete detail; the intermixture of the strange with the familiar; the imposition of a system of rules or laws; and the use of invented maps and histories. Stories of imaginary worlds tend, for example, to be rich in detail. Child psychologist Lili Peller has even suggested that the use of such detail in fantasy may account for the fascination of the genre; she explains that the denial of everyday reality is combined with "highly realistic and prosaic details which in a way deny the first denial. The reader is shuttled between the two, and this double denial may account for the story's ability to hold his interest."[5]

Historical novels and science fiction stories, however, are also characterized by richness of detail, and for the same practical reason; detail enables readers to visualize environments that they have never seen, and lends these environments something of the solidity and richness of texture that characterizes real-life experience. Sensory detail—detail that evokes the five senses—is especially helpful, since what we perceive, often unconsciously, through our ears, nose, and skin convinces us that we are in an environment rather than seeing it from outside. Well-handled sensory detail makes readers feel as if they are sharing the total experience of the characters—seeing, smelling, hearing, and tasting what the characters see, smell, hear, and taste. Concrete detail is detail that increases specificity; it answers such questions as how many? what color? how tall? what did they eat for breakfast? what did he have in his pocket? and is particularly relished by children.

Baum's most conspicuous cluster of sensory details occurs in the first two chapters of *The Wizard,* creating the contrast between gray, dry Kansas and the colorful, fertile world of Oz; his purpose here, as we noted in chapter 5, is not simply to make both places vivid to the imagination but to define them as states of being. Once this has been accomplished, Baum uses concrete and sensory detail to help build his new world, to show readers how different it is from their own, and to enable them to share Dorothy's experiences there. He tells us, for example, that the Munchkin men who greeted Dorothy "wore round hats that rose to a small point a foot above their heads, with little bells around the brims that tinkled sweetly as they moved" (*Wizard,* 12), and that the Munchkin houses "were odd looking dwellings, for each was round, with a big dome for a roof. All were painted blue, for in this country of the East blue was the favorite color" (19). Both the costumes and the houses are unlike those found anywhere in our world; at the same time, being able to visualize the hats and hear the bells gives them a kind of reality in our minds. Similarly, Dorothy sets off for the Emerald City with "her silver shoes twinkling merrily on the hard, yellow roadbed" (18). The concrete and sensory details at once emphasize how odd it is to be wearing silver shoes and help us imagine what walking in them down a yellow brick road might feel like. Baum's style is not highly descriptive nor his choice of words and images especially original compared to those of such writers of fantasy as Kenneth Grahame, J. R. R. Tolkien, Ursula K. Le Guin, or E. B. White, but he provides the kinds of details that children most like to know. In *The Wizard* he supplies no architectural particulars of the Palace of Oz—it is merely "a big building, exactly in the middle of the City" (63)—but he tells young readers exactly what Dorothy's bedroom was like and what she wore for her audience with the Wizard—a gown of "green brocaded satin" and "a green silk apron" (65). He describes interesting processes in detail as well—how the four travelers crossed a ravine (41–42), how the Winkies repaired the Tin Woodman (84–85), how the Wizard and Dorothy constructed their balloon (107)—aware that children are always curious to learn how things are done.

A world different from ours in every possible respect would be incomprehensible to any reader, but adults can handle a higher degree of strangeness than children. Science fiction writers for adults, for example, can and do create future worlds and distant planets far more complex and bizarre than those in children's science fiction. Thus, while all fiction that depicts other worlds necessarily mingles the familiar with the strange, fantasy for children often does so in ways that lead the young reader by easy and gentle degrees into the otherness of another world. C. S. Lewis uses this technique in *The Lion, the Witch and the Wardrobe;* Lucy begins her transition from our world into Narnia in an ordinary wardrobe filled with fur coats, becomes aware that the fur has changed into the prickly needles of evergreens, moves forward into a snowy wood whose only oddity is a lamppost among the trees, and finally sees a faun with an umbrella—at which point, she is clearly in an imaginary world. Although J. R. R. Tolkien sets the entire story of *The Hobbit* in his imaginary world of Middle-earth, he guides the young reader in similar fashion from the familiar into the strange. His protagonist, Bilbo, resembles an ordinary human being and lives in an area of Middle-earth much like the English countryside; together, Bilbo and the reader journey into stranger and stranger places inhabited by creatures less and less like human beings. Even E. B. White begins *Charlotte's Web* like a realistic animal story about a little girl and her pet pig; Wilbur and the other animals do not start talking till midway through chapter 3.

Lewis Carroll, Baum's primary influence, pioneered this technique in the Alice books, both of which begin with an ordinary little girl in familiar surroundings. In *Alice in Wonderland,* Alice is sitting in a meadow when she sees a rabbit run past—not an ordinary brown rabbit, however, but a white rabbit with pink eyes. With a mathematician's precision, Carroll measures the increasing degree of fantasy:

> There was nothing so *very* remarkable in that; nor did Alice think it so *very* much out of the way to hear the Rabbit say to itself, "Oh dear! Oh dear! I shall be too late!" (when she thought it over afterwards, it occurred to her that she ought to have wondered at this, but at the time it all seemed quite natural); but when the Rabbit actually *took a watch out of its waistcoat-pocket,* and looked at it, and then hurried on, Alice started to her feet, for it flashed across her mind that she had never before seen a rabbit with either a waistcoat-pocket, or a watch to take out of it, and, burning with curiosity, she ran across the field after it, and was just in time to see it pop down a large rabbit-hole under the hedge.[6]

In *Through the Looking-Glass,* Alice imagines what it might be like to visit the world she can see in the looking glass. Then she sees the glass turning into a kind of mist, and climbs through the frame into Looking-Glass Country.

Although Baum's cyclone is a more dramatic way to transport a little girl from one world to another, he uses the same step-by-step technique. Nothing could be more depressingly ordinary than the Kansas homestead where the story opens. The cyclone, though extraordinary, belongs to our reality; for a cyclone to pick up a small building and set it down, unharmed, somewhere else is still within the reach of possibility. Even when Dorothy opens the door, the landscape she sees has nothing overtly fantastic in it. The small size and odd costumes of the Munchkins and the Witch of the North are the first clue that Dorothy has landed in another world, and the Witch's hailing her as " 'most noble Sorceress' "(*Wizard,* 12) is the first indication that the world is magical. Other magical elements are also gradually introduced. Dorothy is hesitant to believe that witches exist and that some witches are good, though by the end of the chapter, she has not only "begun to look upon the little old woman as her only friend" but has accepted what she is; when the Witch vanishes, "Dorothy, knowing her to be a witch, had expected her to disappear in just that way, and was not surprised in the least" (17). As with Alice, Lucy, and Bilbo, Dorothy's initiation into the new world enables the reader to be initiated along with her.

Much of what Dorothy experiences in the Land of the Munchkins is basically familiar to her, though with an element of strangeness. The landscape is farming country, though more prosperous and fertile than Kansas and dotted with round blue houses instead of square white ones. The food she eats at Boq's house includes "fruits and nuts, pies and cakes, and many other good things to eat" (19). A scarecrow in a field of corn is a familiar sight. Baum's transformation of this scarecrow into his first nontraditional imaginary being uses increasing degrees of fantasy for a particularly memorable effect. He begins by describing it minutely, mingling details specific to this imaginary world with others that might characterize any American scarecrow:

> Its head was a small sack of stuffed straw, with eyes, nose and mouth painted on it to represent a face. An old, pointed blue hat, that had belonged to some Munchkin, was perched on this head, and the rest of the figure was a blue suit of clothes, worn and faded, which had also been stuffed with straw. On the feet were some old boots with blue tops, such as every man wore in this country, and the figure was raised above the stalks of corn by means of the pole stuck up its back.

> While Dorothy was looking earnestly into the queer, painted
> face of the Scarecrow, she was surprised to see one of the eyes
> slowly wink at her. (21–23)

A wink—the most minimal of movements—is the first sign that the
Scarecrow is alive. The Scarecrow then nods at Dorothy—a more pro-
nounced movement—and finally speaks to her, proving that it is not
only alive but "human."

As she and the Scarecrow travel on together, Dorothy finds herself, like Bilbo, in country that becomes progressively wilder and more
fantastic. Already by chapter 4, "There were fewer houses and fewer
trees, and the farther they went the more dismal and lonesome the
country became" (25). Then comes the dark forest where Dorothy
encounters the Tin Woodman and the Lion, then the monstrous Kalidahs, then the Deadly Poppy Field. Though it represents a return to
civilization, the Emerald City is the most fantastic place of all, with its
dazzling green color and the spectacular magic of the Wizard. By the
final chapters, with his readers fully acclimatized, Baum can develop
his world even further, introducing a whole new race of "human"
beings (the Hammer-Heads) and a separate country within Oz with its
own unique inhabitants (the China Country). In later Oz books, taking as given his readers' knowledge and acceptance of his world, Baum
could plunge his characters with little or no preamble into the midst of
it and give free rein to the invention of new races, cities, countries,
and magic phenomena.

It is not sufficient for a reader's acceptance of an imaginary
world, however, simply to be led gradually into it. The reader must
feel the presence of organizing principles—some order in the imaginary universe—if strange events and characters are not to seem wholly
arbitrary. Again, this holds especially true for young readers. Perhaps
the main reason that *Alice in Wonderland* is disliked by many children
is that its world seems so chaotic, particularly in the first few chapters;
Alice spends much of her time trying to figure out the rules and not
succeeding, though she does learn eventually how to control her
alarming changes of size. In "Modern Fairy Tales" Baum himself called
Carroll's story "rambling and incoherent" and complained that "the

story may often bewilder the little one—for it is bound to bewilder us, having neither plot nor motive in its relation" (Hearn 1983, 138–39). The physical design of Wonderland is equally incoherent, as anyone will discover who tries to make a map of it or to trace the route of Alice's adventures.

The first author of fantasy to suggest that an imaginary world should operate by its own self-consistent set of principles was Lewis Carroll's friend George MacDonald, in his essay "The Fantastic Imagination":

> The natural world has its laws, and no man must interfere with them in the way of presentment any more than in the way of use; but they themselves may suggest laws of other kinds, and man may, if he pleases, invent a little world of his own, with its own laws; for there is that in him which delights in calling up new forms—which is the nearest, perhaps, he can come to creation. . . .
>
> His world once invented, the highest law that comes next into play is, that there shall be harmony between the laws by which the new world has begun to exist; and in the process of his creation, the inventor must hold by those laws. The moment he forgets one of them, he makes the story, by its own postulates, incredible. To be able to live a moment in an imagined world, we must see the laws of its existence obeyed. Those broken, we fall out of it. The imagination in us, whose exercise is essential to the most temporary submission to the imagination of another, immediately, with the disappearance of Law, ceases to act.[7]

For MacDonald, a devout Christian, the need to govern imaginary worlds by Law had spiritual significance, being rooted in the nature of the universe—itself the creation of God: "Obeying laws, the maker works like his creator; not obeying law, he is such a fool as heaps a pile of stones and calls it a church" (163). He emphasized that the freedom to invent new laws applied only to the realm of nature, not to that of morality:

> In the moral world it is different: there a man may clothe in new forms, and for this employ his imagination freely, but he must invent nothing. He may not, for any purpose, turn its laws upside

down. He must not meddle with the relations of live souls. The laws of the spirit of man must hold, alike in this world and in any world he may invent. (163–64)

Not all authors today would agree with MacDonald on this point, but it is true that questions of morality often seem less complex or debatable in imaginary worlds than in the world we know. Authors often assume a simple and traditional moral structure, whether because it seems more appropriate to a genre in which Good and Evil may assume tangible form, or for practical reasons; with so much that is already strange, a new or very complex system of morality might be too much to digest—or simply too distracting—for the reader.

Whether or not Carroll discussed the creation of imaginary worlds with MacDonald, his Looking-Glass Country is far easier for Alice and for the reader to comprehend than Wonderland—particularly for the reader who knows the rules of chess, which govern its physical design and much of what happens there. In addition, the Red Queen gives Alice a view of the world from a hilltop before she begins her journey, and tells her the route to take. This appears to have been Baum's model for chapter 2 in *The Wizard,* in which the Witch of the North and the Munchkins explain the geography of Oz and instruct Dorothy to follow the yellow brick road. Dorothy is also told of the five figures who wield power in Oz; since these consist of four Witches and a Wizard, it is clear that their power derives from magic.

In an imaginary world, the natural laws that rule our world no longer necessarily hold true, and things that are impossible in our world become possible through what is loosely called "magic." Thus, it is crucial that magic show the same degree of logic and consistency in an imaginary world that natural laws do in ours. Magical beings like dragons and fairies must act according to their natures, magical objects must work by certain rules, and witches and sorcerers must have limited and defined powers; a world in which a wizard could simply "do anything" would lose all credibility—and interest—for the reader. Baum possessed the kind of mind that enjoys playing by such rules, and although he did not work out all the ramifications of his new world in *The Wizard,* there is already a basic consistency in the way its magic functions. One of his primary assumptions, as Hugh Pendexter points out, is that "magic works only when performed in a fairy country. The silver shoes cannot even enter the 'civilized' world, and while the Magic Belt can transport Dorothy from Kansas to Oz, the Belt must be in Oz to work."[8] Ruth Plumly Thompson and other followers of Baum failed to observe this limitation, blurring the distinction between Oz and our world.

Baum also distinguishes carefully in his later Oz books between fairy magic (which fairies perform simply by virtue of being fairies) and the magic practiced by witches, sorcerers, and magicians. Because fairies, in Baum's mythology, are virtuous beings, fairy magic is always beneficent; the enchantment that makes Oz a "fairyland" and protects its inhabitants from age, sickness, and (in most cases) death is the result of fairy magic. Only the type of magic employed by witches and magicians, however—and the purely illusionary magic of the Wizard—is shown actively at work in *The Wizard of Oz*. Historically, magic and science sprang from the same root—the desire to control nature—and it is not difficult to imagine a world in which what we may call a "scientific" magic performs many of the functions performed by science in ours. Oz, though one of the earliest to be developed, is only one of many such worlds in fantasy and science fiction.[9] Such magic, like science, is morally neutral; it is, as Pendexter describes it, "a science which any knowledgable person can learn and apply for good or evil according to his nature" (2). A scientific magician can learn magic from books, augment it by means of carefully recorded experiments, and produce precise and predictable results; Baum depicts such magicians experimenting with new spells in *The Magic of Oz* and *The Patchwork Girl of Oz*. After Ozma, a fairy, assumes the throne of Oz, the practice of scientific magic is forbidden—the only exceptions being Glinda and the Wizard, who becomes Glinda's apprentice—with the object of keeping this tremendous source of power in safe hands.

A magical object like the Silver Shoes or the Golden Cap is "scientific" rather than "fairy," since it will perform for anyone who knows the correct words and gestures, and will not perform without them.[10] The Witch of the North, for example, does not possess the knowledge to release the power of the Silver Shoes: " '[T]here is some charm connected with them,' "she tells Dorothy, " 'but what it is we never knew' "(*Wizard*, 15). Only Glinda can give Dorothy the information she needs to make them work. The Golden Cap illustrates this principle even more clearly: Dorothy learns the words to control it simply by reading them from the inside of the Cap itself, and the Winged Monkeys obey her as readily as they did the Witch. The strict limitations characteristic of scientific magic are also demonstrated by the Cap, which will give each of its owners only three wishes. As is generally the case, a mistaken wish cannot be recalled, and Dorothy wastes one of hers when she asks the Monkeys to carry her home to Kansas.

For Brian Attebery, a historian of fantasy, Baum's system of magical law not only helps to create consistency in his imaginary world but reveals its "ethical and philosophical substructure." Attebery lists the basic "magical operations" Baum uses as "animation, transformation, illusion, disillusion, transportation [by magical means], protection, and luck" (104). Animation, for example, is a frequent occurrence in Oz, bringing to life not only the Scarecrow but Jack Pumpkinhead, the Patchwork Girl, the Glass Cat, and many other characters. As Attebery points out, the end result is nearly always positive in Baum's scheme of things: "These animations are part of a general tendency toward increasing richness of life; they represent a universe slanted toward Becoming" (105). Transformation, on the other hand, is generally bad if it involves imposing "a new shape on an unwilling victim" but good if it involves restoring someone to his or her original form. Illusion and disillusion form another opposing pair; again, "[T]he operation that denies reality is evil, and that which restores it is good" (106). Illusion is often easily overthrown—as Toto unmasks the Wizard—suggesting that evil exists only in the mind. Protection (the kiss given Dorothy by the Good Witch) and luck are closely related, providing yet another expression of the fundamental goodness of Baum's world. The laws governing the performance of magic in Oz thus help to define a universe not only ordered but biased toward beneficence.

The single most essential law—here Baum would have agreed with George MacDonald—is that good is more powerful than evil.

Glinda searches her records in *The Marvelous Land of Oz* (Chicago: Reilly and Britton, 1904). The massive volumes in John R. Neill's illustration suggest the accumulated power of Glinda's knowledge.

The leader of the Winged Monkeys openly admits this when he sees the mark of the Good Witch's kiss on Dorothy's forehead: " 'We dare not harm this little girl ... for she is protected by the Power of Good, and that is greater than the Power of Evil' " (*Wizard*, 79). In *The Life and Adventures of Santa Claus,* much of which deals with a struggle between good and evil powers, Baum states this principle even more strongly; it is, he says, "the Law that while Evil, unopposed, may accomplish terrible deeds, the powers of Good can never be overthrown when opposed to Evil."[11] For him, this was not merely the appropriate cosmic view for a fairy tale, but a matter of deep personal conviction.

A sense of logic operating even in minor details strengthens the reader's trust in an imaginary world, and becomes a source of enjoyment in itself. At one point, for example, the Scarecrow tells Dorothy that the only thing in the world he fears is a lighted match (*Wizard*, 24), and although Baum makes no further use of this information, its logic satisfies the reader. If a scarecrow stuffed with straw could come to life, it might well be invulnerable to hunger or cold or predatory animals but be more vulnerable than we are to the threat of fire. Conversely, the Wicked Witch of the West, for whom the touch of water is deadly, always carries an umbrella in her hand (81); and the sudden dissolution into dust of the Wicked Witch of the East suggests that an old and wicked witch may be as dry inwardly as she is externally.[12] Baum's oddest characters—such original creations as the Scarecrow, the Tin Woodman, the Patchwork Girl, the Glass Cat, Tik-Tok, the Wogglebug, and the Woozy—are never allowed to degenerate into human beings in costume; their uniqueness continues to display itself in the details of what they say, how they behave, and how they view the world. When Dorothy and her friends arrive at Glinda's Castle, for example, each prepares for the formal audience in her or his own fashion: "Dorothy washed her face and combed her hair, and the Lion shook the dust out of his mane, and the Scarecrow patted himself into his best shape, and the Woodman polished his tin and oiled his joints" (128).

Baum's attention to detail and to the internal logic of his world makes something memorable even of a little girl's dress:

> Dorothy had only one other dress, but that happened to be clean
> and was hanging on a peg beside her bed. It was gingham, with
> checks of white and blue; and although the blue was somewhat
> faded with many washings, it was still a pretty frock. The girl
> washed herself carefully, dressed herself in the clean gingham,
> and tied her pink sunbonnet on her head. (18)

The concrete details of this passage are included not only because
young readers will enjoy hearing them, and because they say something about the poverty of Dorothy's family and her ability to take
care of herself, but for the special significance of Dorothy's dress a little later in the chapter. When Boq, her Munchkin host, sees her Silver
Shoes, he remarks,

> "You must be a great sorceress."
> "Why?" asked the girl.
> "Because you wear silver shoes and have killed the wicked
> witch. Besides, you have white in your frock, and only witches
> and sorceresses wear white."
> "My dress is blue and white checked," said Dorothy, smooth-
> ing out the wrinkles in it.
> "It is kind of you to wear that," said Boq. "Blue is the color of
> the Munchkins, and white is the witch color; so we know you are
> a friendly witch."
> Dorothy did not know what to say to this, for all the people
> seemed to think her a witch, and she knew very well she was only
> an ordinary little girl who had come by the chance of a cyclone
> into a strange land. (19–21)

This conversation underlines the paradox of Dorothy's innocence and
the power she manifests in Oz. It reinforces the otherness of Oz, asking us to imagine a world in which a faded blue and white gingham
dress can send a vital message. It emphasizes the importance of color
in Baum's imaginary world, while demonstrating that colors have different meanings there than they do for us. The passage is doubly effective because its "facts" can be checked against other passages in *The
Wizard.* Mentions of blue as "the color of the Munchkins" are frequent in the first few chapters, and Baum does not forget that "white

is the witch color"; the Good Witch of the North wore "a white gown that hung in plaits from her shoulders" (12), and Glinda's dress, many chapters later, is "pure white" (128) as well.[13]

Maps—a real-life kind of magic—provide yet another means of heightening the reality of an imaginary world. Normally we accept maps as objective and trustworthy guides, assuming a one-to-one correspondence between the points on the map and the physical features of the territory. The very existence of a map implies the existence of a place to correspond with it. But in books, maps are most effective as a stimulus to the imagination. Robert Louis Stevenson drew a map, labeled it "Treasure Island," and saw it come alive with a story of pirates and buried gold. Maps designed to accompany narratives—whether they picture a mere floor plan in a murder mystery, the route of an expedition, or an entire world—provide more than convenient landmarks; they invite readers to become active participants. We are encouraged to locate ourselves inside the story by finding where we "are" at a given moment, where we have been, and where we might go next. Maps of imaginary worlds do even more, enlarging the world beyond the boundaries of the story. On the map, above the particular mountain our protagonist is climbing, we can see an entire mountain range extending northward, and our awareness that the range is there adds depth to the world, even if—or perhaps especially if—the story never takes us there. The detailed maps included in *The Hobbit* and *The Lord of the Rings* expand the geography of Middle-earth far beyond the places visited by the characters, just as in real life we are aware of a far larger world than the small area we inhabit or journey through. Today most stories of imaginary worlds include a map or aerial view; some stories that did not originally come with maps, such as *The Wind in the Willows* and the Chronicles of Narnia, have since acquired them.[14]

Children who invent imaginary worlds draw maps of them, as if by instinct; the Brontë children had their map of Angria, drawn and colored by Branwell, and the young C. S. Lewis his map of Animal Land. Baum, who never illustrated his own work and who had so few predecessors in the creation of a fully developed imaginary world, does not seem to have realized at first how useful a map would be for Oz, though his precise description in *The Wizard* shows that he had one in his head from the beginning. The earliest known map of Oz was designed as one of the colored slides for his stage production *Fairylogue and Radio Plays* and dates from 1908 to 1909 (shown in Hearn 1973, 33). Although Baum had written several Oz books by this time and evolved a complex world, the map is a very simple one. Oz is square and surrounded by an even border labeled "Desert" on all four sides. The four realms are shaped roughly like equilateral triangles colored blue (Munchkins), red (Quadlings), yellow (Winkies), and (oddly enough) pale green (Gillikins), with a large green circle labeled Emerald City in the center. A star marks the spot where Dorothy's house landed, and a dotted line traces the yellow brick road. Glinda's Castle in the far south is the other notable landmark.

In 1914, two much more elaborate full-color maps of Oz, supposedly drawn by Professor Wogglebug, T. E., appeared in *Tik-Tok of Oz* (shown in Hearn 1973, 386). One was a map of Oz and the surrounding desert; the other extended to the countries beyond the desert (including countries in Baum's non-Oz fantasies) and the Nonestic Ocean surrounding the entire continent. These maps are rectangular, spread across two pages, and their irregular borders give them a more realistic appearance. The desert that surrounds Oz is now called the Deadly Desert (its most common name) to the east, the Impassable Desert to the north, and the Great Sandy Waste to the south; to the west, it is called the Shifting Sands. All the major lakes, rivers, mountain ranges, forests, and dwellings mentioned in the Oz books to that date are included, with a large cross to mark "Where Dorothy's House Fell." There is, however, one very serious flaw. Somehow Professor Wogglebug has reversed the directions so clearly specified in *The Wizard* and placed the Munchkin Country in the west and the Winkie Country in the east. In its original form, as first published, the compass directions were also reversed, with the "E" on the left and the "W" on the right, thus correcting the error; when the map was republished, however, the "E" and "W" were returned to their normal positions, while the Munchkin and Winkie Countries were left reversed. Since Baum (and later Thompson) used this version for reference in later Oz books, the original error was compounded each time new locations were added—creating a virtually insoluble problem for cartographers.

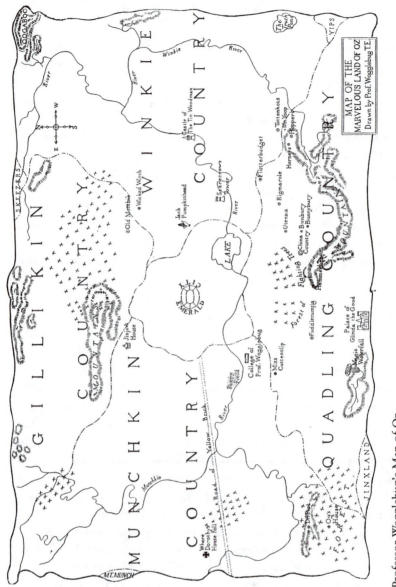

Professor Wogglebug's Map of Oz.
*By John R. Neill, originally published in* Tik-Tok of Oz *(Chicago: Reilly and Britton, 1914).*

(The small kingdom of Oogaboo first mentioned in *Tik-Tok of Oz,* for example, is found on some maps in the extreme northwest and on others in the extreme northeast of Oz, sometimes in the Munchkin Country and sometimes in the Winkie Country.) The official map of Oz created for the International Wizard of Oz Club by James E. Haff and Dick Martin returns to the original configuration described in *The Wizard* and used by Baum himself in *Fairylogues and Radio Plays.*[15]

Whatever the difficulties caused by the Wogglebug, the detailed maps of Oz became a new source of fascination for young readers. *The Lost Princess of Oz* (1915) featured a special map of its own, on which one could find the locations mentioned in the story and trace the routes of the two groups of travelers.

Just as a map expands the reality of an imaginary world in space, the history of an imaginary world expands its reality in time. The allusions to ancient feuds and wars in *The Hobbit* and the vast span of Narnian history, extending back to its creation, make it possible to imagine that Middle-earth and Narnia exist in their own right, independently of the particular story being told. Baum had given little thought to this aspect of world creation when he wrote *The Wizard of Oz,* though he took the process a step further than Lewis Carroll, whose imaginary worlds, being dreams, naturally have neither past nor future. The Wizard does relate to Dorothy and her companions how he first came to Oz and supervised the building of the Emerald City—explaining the anomalies of a wizard from Omaha and an Emerald City that isn't green after all. Baum also supplies a history for the Golden Cap, most of which Dorothy learns from the King of the Flying Monkeys on her way to Glinda's Castle. Although commentators have condemned this tale as extraneous to the main narrative, it is an interesting early experiment at developing a history for Oz. " 'That was many years ago,' " says the Monkey, " 'long before Oz came out of the clouds to rule over this land' "(92); this single sentence tells the reader that Oz was not created when Dorothy opened the door, but extends backward into its own time past.

*The Wizard* was not originally intended to have a sequel; when Baum went on to write *The Land of Oz* (1904), he began for the first time to think about the history of his world—how it had become enchanted, who had ruled Oz before the Wizard came, how the Wizard was able to seize the throne, and what might have become of the rightful heir (Ozma, who takes her place as ruler of Oz at the end of the story). He was still inventing Oz history on an ad hoc basis rather than planning it systematically, so that certain inconsistencies (in the character of the Wizard, for example) remain to puzzle readers. On the other hand, as the series grew, a post-*Wizard* history evolved naturally with it. Rather than using new characters like Tik-Tok or the Patchwork Girl only once, Baum allowed them to accumulate, book by book; the result is that children reading one of the later books find themselves in a crowd of old friends sharing common memories. This, perhaps, is what contributes most to the sense of Oz as a place that exists independently of its historians.

This analysis of Baum's techniques helps to explain what makes Oz a convincing imaginary world—and a particularly impressive one given the dearth of models Baum had to draw upon. But we also need to ask what is distinctive about Oz among the other worlds of this kind, how to account for its distinctive characteristics, and what their significance may be—beginning with the most obvious components of its outer landscape, the use of shape and color as fundamental principles of design.

Oz is shaped like a rectangle divided into triangular quadrants, with the Emerald City at the center and a border of desert encircling the whole. Each of the areas is associated with a different color, the three countries mentioned in *The Wizard* with the three primary colors. In the eastern Munchkin Country the color is blue; in the western Winkie Country, yellow; in the southern Quadling Country, red; and in the northern Gillikin Country (as we learn in *The Land of Oz*), purple. The Emerald City, of course, is green. As the four travelers enter the Quadling Country,

> The fences and houses and bridges were all painted bright red, just as they had been painted yellow in the country of the Winkies and blue in the country of the Munchkins. The Quadlings themselves, who were short and fat and looked chubby and good natured, were dressed all in red, which showed bright against the green grass and the yellowing grain. (*Wizard*, 127)

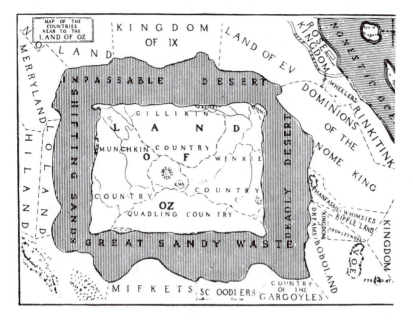

Map of the countries surrounding Oz. Several of these countries originate in non-Oz fantasies by Baum, including *Queen Zixi of Ix* (1905) and *Dot and Tot of Merryland* (1901).
*By John R. Neill, originally published in* Tik-Tok of Oz *(Chicago: Reilly and Britton, 1914).*

Even the vegetation is influenced by the prevailing color. On their way back from the Yellow Castle in the Winkie Country, for example, Dorothy and her friends pass through "big fields of buttercups and yellow daisies" (88). In *The Land of Oz,* Baum carried this a step further; Tip explains that in the Gillikin Country, " '[T]he grass is purple, and the trees are purple and the houses and fences are purple.... Even the mud in the road is purple' "(35). This was a difficult idea to sustain, however, and is inconsistently applied in later books.[16]

Oz was not the only imaginary land of Baum's with this basic shape. Yew, in *The Enchanted Island of Yew* (1903), is a round island divided into four kingdoms shaped like the slices of a pie—Dawna in the east, Auriel in the west, Plenta in the south, and Heg in the north—with a fifth kingdom, Spor, in the exact center. Such a shape—

a quartered space with a central axis—occurs in many mythologies as a symbol for the world itself. The "four quarters of the earth" represent the four directions (east, west, north, and south), while the central axis unites them all in harmony. In Buddhist depictions, the *axis mundi* or World Navel is the place of the Bo Tree where Buddha experienced enlightenment; on medieval maps, the axis mundi is Jerusalem. Carl Jung uses this shape to represent his concept of the Self, the ordering and unifying center of the total psyche. Often the four regions are each assigned a different color. In ceremonial Navajo sand paintings, some of which bear a remarkable resemblance to the maps of Yew and Oz, the colors of the four quadrants are white (east), blue (west), yellow (south), and black (north); in the small circle at the center may stand the figure of a god—just as the mysterious Wizard and then the fairy Ozma occupy the Emerald City at the center of Oz. In the 1890s, Baum had developed an interest in Theosophy, a religion of spiritual search founded in 1875 that drew from several Eastern religions—particularly Buddhism and Hinduism. Although Baum did not accept all the teachings of Theosophy, it appealed to his tolerant spirit, and it is possible that in the process of learning about Eastern religions, he discovered these archetypal images.[17]

Another possible source for the design of Oz, however, lay in his own childhood, when he wandered through the gardens of Rose Lawn—the lost Paradise he recaptured by creating Oz. "In every direction," he writes of Rose Lawn, "were winding paths covered with white gravel, which led to all parts of the grounds, looking for all the world like a map" (Hearn 1973, 12). The map of Oz does resemble a Victorian garden, typically symmetrical, with flower beds each of a different color and a central summerhouse or gazebo in a circular green lawn from which to survey the whole—much the same sort of garden, in fact, that Baum designed for himself when he moved to Hollywood. Shaped like a rectangle 100 feet wide by 125 feet deep, the garden at "Ozcot" contained a central summerhouse, where Baum wrote his stories; and a circular aviary nearby contained a running fountain and several hundred colorful songbirds. Here, then, were all the elements of Oz as Dorothy first sees it—grass, trees, flowers, singing birds, and flowing water. "In memory of the formal gardens of

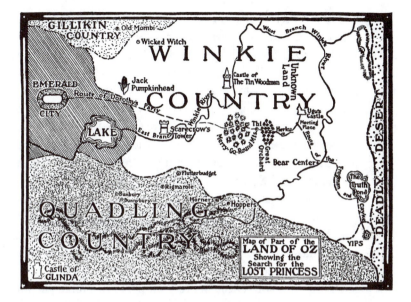

A map published in *The Lost Princess of Oz* (Chicago: Reilly and Britton, 1917).

his childhood home," his biographers tell us, Baum planted symmetrically arranged flower beds in single varieties of flowers—such brilliantly colored flowers as delphiniums, oriental poppies, snapdragons, and marigolds (Baum and MacFall, 268–69).

It is not surprising that color played so powerful a role in his concept of Oz, for a love of strong, bright color was characteristic of Baum all his life. Long before Oz, he jokingly told one of his sons that he was going to buy him a "combination suit"—a combination, that is, of "green pants, yellow coat, purple hat and blue shirt" (Baum and MacFall, 82). In "Our Landlady," the column he wrote for his newspaper in drought-stricken Aberdeen, Baum described how one farmer fooled his starving horses into eating wood shavings instead of grass— by fitting them with green goggles (74). Green seems to have been a favorite of his; at Ozcot he used pale green stationery and made lighting fixtures for the dining room that filtered the light through emerald green glass (265). His original name for *The Wizard of Oz,* as we have noted, was *The Emerald City,* and despite the protests of publishers that color printing was too expensive for a full-length story, he and Denslow insisted on color illustrations throughout. In a letter just prior to its publication, Baum wrote with satisfaction, "Denslow has made profuse illustrations for it and it will glow with bright colors" (119). The colors of the illustrations were keyed to the colors of the various regions in Oz; Baum used a similar device in *The Road to Oz* (1909), in which the illustrations were in black and white but the paper changed color as the characters visited different countries. The concept of color theming particularly fascinated him, and in *The Wizard* he transformed the sardonic joke from "Our Landlady" into a city color-themed in green. As the Wizard explains to Dorothy, " 'Then I thought, as the country was so green and beautiful, I would call it the Emerald City, and to make the name fit better I put green spectacles on all the people, so that everything they saw was green' "(100).

Baum's use of color reflects more than personal preference; at the turn of the century, color theming was the latest trend, from interior decoration, department store displays, and dinner parties, to the White City of the Chicago Fair. A fashionable hostess might give a "Snow Luncheon" in which everything was white—tablecloth, china, candles, flowers, even an all-white menu including cream of chicken soup, cod with oyster sauce, creamed potatoes, "snowball cakes" rolled in coconut, and coffee with whipped cream. And color theming was only the beginning. Hostesses vied with each other to create original party themes. *Entertainments for All Seasons* (1904) informs its readers how to give a Butterfly Party, a Lemon Party, a Peanut Party, an Evening in Ye Forest of Arden, a Mexican Luncheon, a Knickerbocker Tea Party, a Corn Social, and many more—with invitations, decorations, costumes, games, and menus to fit the themes.[18] Baum's own vacation home in Michigan, built with his earnings from *Father Goose,* had a goose theme: "The Sign of the Goose" was decorated with a goose-shaped rocking chair, a frieze of green geese, which Baum stenciled himself, around the living room, and a brightly colored window with a goose in stained glass (Gardner and Nye, 24).

This popular trend and the unaffected pleasure Baum found in it helps explain one of the most distinctive features of his imaginary world—the existence within Oz of innumerable small towns and countries, each based on a single concept logically developed—in fact, a theme. The first of these was the China Country in *The Wizard,* which Dorothy and her friends discover on their journey to Glinda's Castle. Here, surrounded by a high wall, is a land whose people and animals are small china figurines come to life; even the ground is "as smooth and shining and white as the bottom of a big platter" (117). The travelers cross this country very carefully, afraid of breaking the brittle little people, who run fearfully away from them. Every Oz book contains at least one of these autonomous communities; in *The Road to Oz* and *The Emerald City of Oz,* visiting such places becomes an end in itself. In *The Emerald City,* for example, Dorothy visits Bunbury (in which the entire town and its inhabitants are breads, cakes, etc.), Bunnybury (peopled entirely by rabbits), the land of the Cuttenclips (a paper doll world), Utensia (inhabited by kitchen utensils), and several other odd places. The party stops for lunch at the castle of the Tin Woodman, where the theme is tin—even to the tin flowers in the garden, which "glistened under the sunlight like spun silver" (249). To many adult critics, these episodes are pointless digressions from the main story line, but to children, they may be part of the special appeal of Oz.

Though many adults never outgrow a sneaking fondness for theming, the taste for it is now associated with children, whose birthday parties are still planned around such themes as cowboys, space wars, or the circus. Collecting objects with a common theme—rocks, bottle caps, baseball cards, miniature horses—is another activity most children enjoy. Again, while this taste may carry over into adult life, adults typically justify their collections as having historical, scientific, or monetary value, rather than risk the stigma of being "childish." Dorothy's bedroom in the Emerald City, with its green silk sheets, green books full of green pictures, and wardrobe of green dresses, exactly satisfies children's uninhibited delight in theming. I remember my two small nieces literally bouncing with glee as I told them about a chocolate room with a chocolate bed and chocolate pillows and chocolate sheets. Something about the combination of logic and imagination found in theming seems not merely entertaining but exciting to children—and to Baum.

Much of the appeal of Oz comes from the sheer fertility of invention with which Baum conceived and continued to develop it throughout the series. There are always new realms, new peoples, new inventions, and strange new characters to discover; at the same time, Baum's strong sense of logical consistency—and the logical aspect of theming—prevent the abundance and variety from dissolving into chaos. In *The Magic of Oz*, Baum explains that "[t]his fairyland is so big... that all of it is not yet known to its girl Ruler, and it is said that in some far parts of the country, in forests and mountain fastnesses, in hidden valleys and thick jungles, are people and beasts that know as little about Ozma as she knows of them" (55). Thus the sense of mystery and expectancy is preserved, while the near-omnipotent fairy magic through which Ozma oversees and rules her dominions, emanating from the axis mundi of the Emerald City, continues to maintain the whole in harmony. The map of Oz, whose structure is instantly perceived and comprehended, proclaims an ordered universe within which, nonetheless, not only variety but a degree of disorder can be permitted. Baum's world is analogous to the activity of spontaneous play, in which the exercise of the imagination is not inhibited but freed by the existence of rules agreed upon by the players. The fundamental need for play—not merely a childish but a human need—may account for much of the satisfaction readers find in Oz.

Another possible analogy is Oz as theme park. Whereas the ordinary, old-fashioned amusement park presents a chaotic assortment of unrelated features, the theme park orders these features in a playful way, inviting visitors to imagine themselves in realms in which rides, restaurants, and souvenirs all contribute to the logical development of a theme. Indeed, Baum may have been the first person to conceive of such a park, not only in literary form but in real life. In 1905 a press announcement claimed that he had purchased Pedloe Island, off the coast of southern California, with the intention of turning the entire island into a miniature Oz. According to Martin Gardner, "A palace and statues of leading Oz personages were to be erected, and a monument to Jack Pumpkinhead built on Wizard's Point" (32). Although this announcement was merely a publicity stunt—Pedloe Island itself was a fiction—50 years later, the first theme park was built in southern California by another specialist in fantasy for children. One might even say that a trip to Disneyland is as close as one can come in real life to a trip to Oz.

In several respects, the likeness between the two is striking—even their physical design. Particularly in its simpler original form, Disneyland has the same cloverleaf shape as Oz, with four distinct regions and a central axis; later, like Oz, it was forced to fit more and more small realms into the original design. Each of the four regions has a unifying theme, like the color themes of Baum's countries. Well-known characters from Disney films may be encountered, just as a visitor to Oz might meet the Scarecrow or the Cowardly Lion. Both Oz and Disneyland combine the futuristic with the nostalgic in an optimistic fashion that suggests the possibility of accommodating and enjoying both. Even the rides in Disneyland bear some resemblance to the events in an Oz book; the visitor/reader experiences a series of episodic adventures, stimulating to the imagination and sometimes scary—but not too scary. One must wonder, indeed, whether Oz directly influenced the concept and design of Disneyland; although no direct connection has been found, it is at least suggestive that in 1954—at the same time Disneyland was under construction—Walt Disney bought the movie rights to 11 Oz books that had not yet been filmed.[19]

Some critics of Baum have been troubled by his placing a trickster and a phony—the Wizard—at the center of his imaginary world.[20] The Emerald City itself might be called a fraud, since it is only the Wizard's trickery that makes everything appear green. However, considering Oz in the context of its real-life predecessor, the White City, and its real-life descendant, Disneyland, shows that Baum is not really advocating mass deception. (Indeed, the scene in which the Wizard is unmasked makes the point so strongly that the con man who attempts to rule will be found out in the end that it is frequently alluded to by those who expose corruption.) Like the Emerald City, the White City was something of an illusion; the "staff" of which its buildings were largely constructed had the appearance of marble but not the durability, and the City was slated for demolition once the fair was over. Disneyland, too, is an illusion. The visitor does not really travel by boat through jungle regions, and the wild animals he sees—even the rock formations—are artificial. All illusions, however, are not necessarily evil; indeed, we may find a special pleasure in experiencing an illusion, knowing that it is an illusion, yet choosing to suspend that knowledge and pretend that it is real. The awareness of those who visited the White City that in six months it would vanish like a soap bubble added poignancy to their enjoyment as they strolled among the magnificent buildings. Baum, who was fascinated by illusion all his life—on the stage, in film, in window display—gives readers a similarly multilayered experience in *The Wizard,* first allowing us to "believe in" the illusions of the Wizard, then giving us the pleasure of knowing "how it was done."

In some respects, Disneyland has become a White City for the late twentieth century, particularly in its influence on architecture and urban planning.[21] Disneyland, however, is a permanent—not to say proliferating—construction rather than a temporary one. Here again the analogy with Oz is suggestive. Baum had not originally planned a sequel to *The Wizard;* his Emerald City was intended to be, in a sense, as temporary as the White City that inspired it. When he found himself writing not just one sequel but another, and another, he proceeded to rebuild the City—and his entire world—in more permanent materials. Ozma, an immortal fairy, takes the place of the aging, incompetent Wizard. Oz becomes a true utopia. And the green-lensed glasses are no longer necessary; the Emerald City, under Ozma, becomes all that the Wizard pretended it to be, and more. Although, Baum now tells us, other jewels are used to decorate its houses and palaces, "[I]n the streets and upon the outside of the buildings only emeralds appear, from which circumstance the place is named the Emerald City of Oz" (*Emerald,* 29).

For Baum, the Emerald City acquired a significance that it had not originally possessed; what was little more than an enjoyable excuse for color theming in *The Wizard* became in later volumes his personal vision of the City Beautiful. He repeatedly describes a group of travelers drawing near the City, awed by the gradual revelation of its wonders—in *The Road to Oz,* for example:

> From the top of the high bridge they could see far away the magnificent spires and splendid domes of the superb city, sparkling

like brilliant jewels as they towered above the emerald walls. The shaggy man drew a deep breath of awe and amazement, for never had he dreamed that such a grand and beautiful place could exist—even in the fairyland of Oz. (181)

The most vivid of these descriptions occurs in *The Patchwork Girl,* the volume in which—after a hiatus—Baum had given way to the demands of his young audience and returned to his position of Royal Historian of Oz:

The gates had bars of pure gold, and on either side of each gateway were built high towers, from which floated gay banners. Other towers were set at distances along the walls, which were broad enough for four people to walk abreast upon.

This enclosure, all green and gold and glittering with precious gems, was indeed a wonderful sight to greet our travelers, who first observed it from the top of a little hill; but beyond the wall was the vast city it surrounded, and hundreds of jeweled spires, domes and minarets, flaunting flags and banners, reared their crests far above the towers of the gateways. In the center of the city our friends could see the tops of many magnificent trees.... (184)

There was much to interest them along the roadway, for the houses were now set more closely together and they met a good many people who were coming or going from one place or another. All these seemed happy-faced, pleasant people, who nodded graciously to the strangers as they passed, and exchanged words of greeting.

At last they reached the great gateway, just as the sun was setting and adding its red glow to the glitter of the emeralds on the green walls and spires. Somewhere inside the city a band could be heard playing sweet music; a soft, subdued hum, as of many voices, reached their ears; from the neighboring yards came the low mooing of cows waiting to be milked. (186)

In these final sentences Baum reaches to the height of fantasy, at which the imaginary achieves an intensity comparable to that of reality itself. Perhaps his own absence from the City had enabled him to envision it more clearly than ever before, for he writes here like a man returning from afar to a place he knows and loves.

The other motif of which Baum never seems to tire is the praise of Ozma. "She is said to be the most beautiful girl the world has ever known," he writes, typically, in *The Emerald City,* "and her heart and mind are as lovely as her person" (33). In *The Magic of Oz,* he tells us that "Ozma, the beautiful girl Ruler of the Fairyland of Oz, was a real fairy, and so sweet and gentle in caring for her people that she was greatly beloved by them all. She lived in the most magnificent palace in the most magnificent city in the world, but that did not prevent her from being the friend of the most humble person in her dominions" (241). Yet Ozma, like the autonomous realms within Oz, is a point at which adult critics often part company with Baum's younger fans. Richard Attebery, for example, admits that "Ozma, Polychrome, and the other fairies who show up in Oz from time to time seem unpleasantly dainty to me now, but when I read the Oz books as a child they were among my favorites" (103). Sarah Hayes, who "used to dream about living in the Emerald City," confirms that "[m]y favorite characters were always beautiful maidens, such as Azarine the Red, Polychrome, and Ozma of course!" (1). "Definitely my favorite character is Ozma," agrees 12-year-old Katy Lau (1). Children, more than adults, readily accept Ozma as the central figure of the fully evolved Oz, just as the Emerald City is its central place. The concept of perfection that Ozma embodies seems to children not sentimental or absurd but real and lovable.

Indeed, love and the happiness that love brings emanate unabashed from Ozma and permeate her world. "The Land of Oz is Love," says Ozma simply—or, as Russel B. Nye puts it, Love is the "First Law" of Baum's utopia. "Love in Oz is kindness, selflessness, friendliness—an inner check that makes one act decently toward human beings, animals, plants, fairies, machines, and even one's enemies" (Gardner and Nye, 10–11). Perhaps the saddest character in all the Oz books is the ferryman in *The Lost Princess* who, because of repeated cruelty to animals, was deprived of the ability to understand what they say. " 'I know that in the Land of Oz animals can speak our language, and so can the birds and bugs and fishes; but in *my* ears they sound merely like growls and chirps and croaks' "(194). To the extent of his unloving behavior, the ferryman is self-exiled from Oz.

As an imaginary world, Oz has both an outer landscape, based on such intellectual concepts as logic and consistency, and an inner landscape, based on emotional needs and desires. Baum speaks to both the intellect and the emotions by centering his world on the double image of the City Beautiful, ordered for the good of all, and the ideal ruler, who rules by love. It is not surprising if for many readers this powerful double image acquires spiritual resonance. In the end the Emerald City does become something like a Celestial City, while Ozma—both immortal being and intimate friend—hovers on the brink of the divine.

Indeed, more than one reader has spoken of the power of Baum's world to offer healing consolation. "Oz is that place," writes Ray Bradbury, "ten minutes before sleep, where we bind up our wounds, soak our feet, dream ourselves better, snooze poetry on our lips, and decide that mankind, for all it's snide and mean and dumb, must be given another chance come dawn and a hearty breakfast."[22] The novelist William Lindsay Gresham tells movingly how rereading his old favorite, *The Scarecrow of Oz,* brought him comfort on a night of despair:

> Let no one doubt the magic of Oz, for with the first sentence, it stole from the pages like a warm, folding shawl about the shoulders of a half-frozen wayfarer.... As I read, I realized for the first time how powerfully the Oz chronicles had influenced my life, how many healthy and sturdy values I had gained from Baum. I thrilled to the Scarecrow's heroic facing of the bonfire, and my perspective was restored by his disposal of the wicked witch Blinkie, and King Krewl—victory without vengeance.
>
> Then came a great healing insight, healing for the wound every child suffers when he is told that Oz is not True. It came like a triumphal chorus, an Ode to Joy, that Oz is True—every golden word of it. It is not fiction, but myth—which states greater truths than mathematical formulae can ever encompass, for it glows with the immortal truth that life moves onward and upward, around obstacles and through terrors toward the sun....
>
> At several places in the story, I gave way to tears of gratitude that a world of sanity was returning to me through the remembered pages. I fell asleep before I had quite finished the book but it didn't matter. I knew it by heart anyhow.[23]

"Is Oz Heaven?" a boy asked at a local meeting of the International Wizard of Oz Club. The adults were silent. But there is something unique in Oz among imaginary worlds—a mingling of superabundant creation with all-permeating love, and a child's humor playing over all—that suggests a more than mortal realm. It is said that when L. Frank Baum lay dying, his last words were, "Now we can cross the Shifting Sands."

# 7

# "Toto, I've a Feeling We're Not in Kansas Anymore": The Movie's Oz

The MGM film of *The Wizard of Oz,* which premiered on 12 August 1939, is an acknowledged classic; in 1989, it was one of 25 films declared "national treasures" by the Librarian of Congress. Repeated showings on television, beginning in 1956, have transformed it into a cultural institution. But how does the world of Oz that the film portrays compare with the Oz Frank Baum created? And which provides the more satisfying or enriching experience for children?

No single vision oversaw the transformation of Baum's story into a movie musical.[1] The studio system in effect at MGM guaranteed that the screenplay would be the product of a succession of writers, each of them molding and remolding the story in response to the demands of producers; to this would be added the separate contributions of a director (*The Wizard* had four), composer, songwriter, costume designer, and art director. Official credit for *The Wizard*'s screenplay went to Noel Langley, Florence Ryerson, and Edgar Allan Woolf, who were responsible for the greater part of it, but at one time or another 10 different screenwriters took their turn. Those who left their mark on the final version included William Cannon, Herman J. Mankiewicz (who first suggested a lengthy Kansas prologue and a more dominant role for the Witch), the songwriter Yip Harburg (who wrote the scene in which the Wizard satisfies the desires of the Scarecrow, the Woodman, and the Lion), Jack Mintz, and John Lee Mahin (who provided the final version of the Kansas prologue). At various points in this complex process, it was proposed to have Dorothy rescue a royal Munchkin couple from the Witch, to give the Witch a son named Bulbo, whom she attempts to make king by conquering the Emerald City, to make Dorothy a teenager in love with the farmhand who becomes the Scarecrow, to avoid killing either of the Witches, to eliminate "Over the Rainbow," to make the Witch trick Dorothy into running across a dissolving Rainbow Bridge, and to have the Wizard's balloon punctured in midflight by a woodpecker. Dorothy's silver shoes disappeared from the story, then reappeared, refashioned for Technicolor as ruby slippers. Again and again, the checks and balances of the system reined in the more extravagant suggestions, returning finally to something surprisingly close to Baum's original story. "In the end," as Michael Patrick Hearn concludes in his introduction to the screenplay, "most of the troubles with the script were easily resolved by simply going back to what L. Frank Baum had done in *The Wonderful Wizard of Oz*" (Langley, 24–25).

One should keep in mind that Baum would probably not have been perturbed by Prince Bulbo or the Rainbow Bridge or the woodpecker—or, for that matter, by the film itself, different though it is in several key respects from his book. The 1902 stage musical version of *The Wizard*, which he helped create, not only substituted a cow named Imogen for Dorothy's dog, Toto, and eliminated the Wicked Witch of the West entirely, but gave the much older Dorothy a "love interest" and added a subplot in which Pastoria, the former King of Oz, battles the Wizard for his throne. Much of this version was designed as a vehicle for the comic vaudeville actors Fred A. Stone and David C. Montgomery, who played the Scarecrow and the Tin Woodman—just as much of the byplay in the MGM movie was designed to display the comic talents of Ray Bolger (the Scarecrow), Jack Haley (the Tin Woodman), and Bert Lahr (the Cowardly Lion). Frank Baum had been an actor, a producer, and a playwright long before he became a children's writer, and he was far more concerned with creating a hit musical than remaining faithful to his own story. The three silent Oz movies that his Oz Film Manufacturing Company produced in 1914 and 1915 represented an equally pragmatic attempt to attract a general audience—including "love interest," dance sequences, and pretty chorus girls—though with less financial success than the stage *Wizard*.[2]

The first film version of *The Wizard,* a silent made by Chadwick Pictures in 1925, bore virtually no resemblance to the original story. Dorothy, now a Kansas flapper, is revealed to be the long-lost Queen of Oz; the comic Kansas farmhand who loves her disguises himself as a scarecrow, and he and Prince Kynd save her from marriage with the evil Prime Minister Kruel. When the MGM *Wizard* was being made, its coproducer Mervyn LeRoy asked Maud Baum what she expected the film to be like. "Oh, I suppose there'll be a Wizard in it," she replied, "and a Scarecrow and a Tin Woodman, and maybe a Lion and a character named Dorothy. But that's all I expect, young man. You see, I've lived in Hollywood since 1910" (Langley, 6).

The most significant differences in plot between the MGM *Wizard* and Baum's original story were the development of a lengthy Kansas prologue in which all the main characters from Oz (except Glinda) appear as ordinary people; the much more dominating presence of the Wicked Witch of the West; the elimination of Dorothy's final journey to Glinda's Castle; and the final revelation that Dorothy's trip to Oz was merely a dream. Several of these changes were interrelated. The decision to expand the Witch's role—fully justifiable from a dramatic point of view—meant that her defeat would become the natural climax, and any later developments would seem anticlimactic; thus, Dorothy's final journey became an early casualty. The decision to make Dorothy's adventures and Oz itself a dream also made it logical to introduce Oz characters into the prologue; naturally, Dorothy would dream about the people she knew.

One of the earliest decisions was to film the Kansas sequences in black and white and Oz in color. An underlined paragraph to this effect appears on the first page of Herman Mankiewicz's 17-page treatment:

As discussed, this part of the picture—until the door is flung open after Dorothy has arrived in the land of the Munchkins—will be shot in black and white, but every effort should be made, through tinting, to emphasize the grey nature of the landscape and Dorothy's daily life. (Harmetz, 27)

A sepia tone was applied to the black-and-white film, giving it the look of early silent films or old family photographs. Coproducer Mervyn LeRoy later claimed credit for the idea (28); he had read and loved *The Wizard* as a child, and perhaps the contrast between Kansas and Oz was something that had particularly impressed him. But the change from gray to color does not account for the full impact of the moment when Dorothy opens the door. Art directors Cedric Gibbons and William Horning made imaginative use of other visual elements as well—shape, size, and color harmony—to define the two very different worlds.

The screenplay only minimally describes the scene of the opening shot, in which Dorothy and Toto come hurrying down the road to the farm, fleeing the vengeance of Miss Gulch: "From the foreground a long straight road leads to and past the farm" (Langley, 34). The farm itself is not described at all. Cinematically, however, the setting makes a strong first impression. Its lines are all right-angled horizontals and verticals—the straight road and flat, gray horizon punctuated by the thin, dark lines of barbed-wire fences, telephone poles, and spindly, leafless trees.[3] In his insightful analysis of the film, Salman Rushdie notes the simple geometrical shapes of the farmhouse and its surroundings—"everything is right angles and triangles"—and suggests that throughout *The Wizard* "home and safety are represented by such geometrical simplicity, whereas danger and evil are invariably twisty, irregular, and misshapen. The tornado is just such an untrustworthy, sinuous, shifting shape."[4] But there is nothing homelike or reassuring in the "geometrical simplicity" of Kansas; rather, the grid of thin, dark lines against the gray plain and sky create—as Baum does with words—a visual equivalent for emotional barrenness and depression. (Audiences of the 1930s would have been reminded of recent drought years and all the human suffering associated with the Dust Bowl.) A homestead as poor as the one Baum describes would have created even more powerful images—the Gales' farm in the film is teeming with pigs, chickens, horses, and far too many farmhands—but as Rushdie points out, "[T]he film's Kansas is also more terrifying than the book's because it adds a presence of real evil: the angular Miss Gulch, with a profile that could carve a joint" (96).

The wistful ballad sung by Judy Garland in this bleak setting was nearly dropped from the picture because of the adverse reactions of other MGM producers at the sneak preview. "Why does she sing in a barnyard?" they complained (Harmetz, 81). For the songwriters, however, "Over the Rainbow" summed up the whole point of the prologue and foreshadowed the transition to another world. As Yip Harburg explained it years later to Aljean Harmetz,

> The book had said Kansas was an arid place where not even flowers grew. The only colorful thing Dorothy saw, occasionally, would be the rainbow. I thought that the rainbow could be a bridge from one place to another. A rainbow gave us a visual reason for going to a new land and a reason for changing to color. (81)

The song served another, subtler function as well. Expressing not merely Dorothy's immediate frustration but the universal human longing for a better place, it sent the first clear signal to the audience that the film was not some childish tale of a little girl and her dog but a story with symbolic and universal significance. Every discussion of deeper levels in this film begins here. For Rushdie, for example, the song expresses the tension between the ostensible moral of the film— "There's no place like home"—and its celebration of "the human dream of leaving—a dream at least as powerful as its countervailing dream of roots" (97). At one point, as she sings, Dorothy grasps the rim of a high-standing wheel; the camera does not show the piece of farm machinery the wheel belongs to, only a large, circular segment— rainbow-shaped—one of the few rounded shapes in the right-angled world of Kansas.

The scene in which the tornado slowly advances upon the helpless Dorothy is far more frightening in the film than in the book—as frightening as the scene in which Dorothy becomes the doomed prisoner of the Witch, and a sort of mirror image of it. There is, as

Rushdie intimates, a visual likeness between the dark, twisted tornado and the dark, crooked Witch, only instead of being locked *inside* the Witch's tower, Dorothy is locked out of the storm cellar. In both scenes, alone and terrified, she cries to Aunt Em for help, in vain. The flying people and animals she sees a little later, through the window of the floating house, though humorous, are not really comforting. Unlike Baum's levelheaded and fully conscious Dorothy, the film's Dorothy is hallucinating, and her delirium turns to nightmare when she sees Miss Gulch peddling past the window on her bicycle. The transformation of Miss Gulch into a witch on a broomstick deftly foreshadows her reappearance as Dorothy's enemy in Oz, but also warns the audience that Oz—however beautiful at first glance—will not be the trouble-free land Dorothy has been yearning for.

The setting into which Dorothy opens the door, described in far more detail than any other in the screenplay, is closely modeled on Baum's description, with its grass, trees, flowers, birds, and flowing stream:

> As DOROTHY opens the door slowly and peers out, a blaze of color greets her. THIS IS THE FIRST TIME WE SEE TECHNI-COLOR. The Kansas scenes were all sepia washes. The inside of the door is monochrome, to give more contrast. When the door is open, the country is shown—a picture of bright greens and blues.

> As DOROTHY goes through the door, the CAMERA TRUCKS after her and then, over her shoulder, to a FULL SHOT of the MUNCHKIN COUNTRY. It is composed of sweeping hills and valleys and dips and waves in the ground; the grass is spangled with daisies; flowers grow everywhere, three or four times life-size, so that hollyhocks stand several feet in the air. The sky is bright blue with little white clouds; and a little stream runs near with huge lily pads on it.

> Feeding the stream is an exquisite fountain. Surrounding the fountain are three or four steps, and to the back of it is Munchkinland's CIVIC CENTER, a quaint little piece of architecture. This is all close to the house in which Dorothy fell from Kansas.

> The scene is quite empty of all signs of life, except the twittering
> of a bird or two in the distance. (Langley, 52)[5]

Looking around her "with an expression of delighted amazement," Dorothy exclaims, "Toto, I've a feeling we're not in Kansas anymore. . . . We must be over the rainbow!" (53).

The screenplay described a landscape of "sweeping hills and valleys and dips and waves in the ground," clearly meant to contrast with the flat prairie landscape of the opening. Gibbons and Horning developed this suggestion into a coherent visual statement about the nature of Oz. In Kansas, horizontal and vertical lines created sharp, angular geometrical forms. In Munchkinland, the geometrical forms are circles and spheres—gentle, rounded forms associated with the nurturing maternal body. The flowers we see as Dorothy opens the door are hollyhocks, with large round blossoms. In the distance are gently rolling hills. The yellow brick road curves round in front of the Civic Center, with its mushroomlike buildings, into a red and yellow spiral that Dorothy traces on foot when she begins her journey. On the other side of the spiral is a round pool with round lily pads floating in it, and a curved bridge crosses the stream. The screenplay mentions "an exquisite fountain" with "three or four steps," without specifying the shape of either. In the Gibbons-Horning set, the steps are three concentric circles rising from the rim of the circular pool; the fountain takes the form of a giant flower, its stem bent in a semicircle, with a rounded bell. Even the Munchkins are short and round—their costumes designed by Adrian to make them look even shorter than they are—as close to little spheres as it is possible for human beings to be. Glinda, of course, arrives in a spherical bubble and wears a floor-length dress whose skirt describes a perfect hemisphere.

Complementing these shapes is a color scheme consisting mainly of soft blues, greens, rose pink, and peach. The effect is gentler than the "blaze of color" specified in the screenplay, except for the rather garish yellow of the road. As the camera lingers over and explores this landscape, before any of its inhabitants appear, the combined shapes and colors speak for themselves, telling us that Oz is essentially a gentle, cheerful, kindly place—a kind of topographical Good Mother.

The appearance of Glinda, the Good Mother figure in both the book and the movie, brings this sequence to its logical climax.

At the same time, there is also the suggestion that this lovely place is less real than Kansas. The flowers shown in close-up as Dorothy steps out through the door are obviously plastic. The stylized landscape is clearly a painted backdrop. The yellow brick road cannot be real brick; it is some flat, shiny substance that looks as artificial as the flowers. Since the masters of illusion at MGM could have created an appearance of photographic realism had they wished to do so, the effect of artificiality must be deliberate—which is entirely logical if one keeps in mind that (although the audience may not yet realize it) Dorothy's adventure is only a dream. The plastic flowers proclaim, from the outset, that the entire world is unreal; in place of the natural beauty Baum describes, we are given a stylized, artificial garden whose inhabitants do not speak normally, but sing or speak in rhyme. Children, however, are much less likely to notice this than adults. Adults know already that Oz is imaginary. Children, wanting to believe in the reality of Oz, see the flowers as real flowers, only bigger and shinier than the flowers of our world.

If the Munchkinland sequence intimates that Oz, though beautiful, is unreal, later scenes suggest that it is also less benign than it appears to be—even less benign, perhaps, than Kansas. After Dorothy's meeting with the Scarecrow, for example, comes the scene in the orchard in which she picks a fine red apple, only to have the apple tree snatch it back and slap her. "Oh, dear! I keep forgetting I'm not in Kansas," says Dorothy, and this time she says it "woefully" (Langley, 70). The Wicked Witch of the West, after her volcanic eruption into the celebration in Munchkinland, seems to be everywhere—lurking near the apple orchard, throwing a fireball at the Scarecrow from the roof of the Tin Woodman's cottage, watching Dorothy and her friends in her crystal ball and plotting something "with poison in it, but attractive to the eye and soothing to the smell!" (82). In the foreground of our first view of the Emerald City, the poisonous poppy field lies like a trap set to spring, with the City as its bait. This time evil wears the disguise of beauty; the gently rolling landscape, the flowers, and the colors—blue, green, and pink—create a treacherous reprise of Munchkinland. Despite the background chorus of Optimistic Voices singing "You're out of the woods / You're out of the dark / You're out of the night" (86), the Emerald City itself is darkened by the Witch flying overhead, skywriting in a trail of black smoke, "Surrender Dorothy," and throwing the entire population into a panic. Having finally reached the City, Dorothy is not safe even there.

Designing the Emerald City posed more problems for Gibbons and Horning than Munchkinland because they had less to go on. Baum does not describe the City in much detail, and most of his ideas had been discarded; in the movie, for example, Dorothy does not spend the night in the green bedroom, and the travelers and inhabitants do not wear the green glasses that were a key point for Baum. In the original edition of *The Wizard,* William Denslow had included a small illustration of the City, which the art directors found too ordinary (Harmetz, 215). The screenplay does not describe the City at all. According to Harmetz, "[S]ketch after sketch of the Emerald City was rejected" (212). At last, Gibbons turned up something in MGM's research library—

> a tiny, a really minuscule photograph of a sketch that had been done in Germany pre-World War I.... We looked at the sketch— it actually looked like test tubes upside down—and it crystallized our ideas.... We all thought the German sketch was right because it wasn't detailed. It didn't look like Rheims Cathedral. It didn't look like the Pyramids. It didn't look like King Tut's Tomb. It looked like some strange thing we had never seen before. (Jack Martin Smith, quoted in Harmetz, 215)

The futuristic style of the sketch helped determine what the inside of the City would look like as well—a kind of streamlined Art Deco with relatively little detail, entirely different from the cluttered, old-fashioned look of Munchkinland.

In view of Baum's own evolving concept of the Emerald City, it is interesting that the MGM writers and designers never seem to have clarified for themselves what the City should represent. Whereas Munchkinland and the Witch's Castle each have their own distinct and consistent character, the City is visually and symbolically a hodgepodge, unified mainly by its color scheme. The futuristic Art Deco setting bears no relationship to the costumes, which themselves range from elaborate quasi-European peasant dresses like those in Munchkinland, to Near Eastern head veils, to the "OZ" T-shirts worn in the "Wash & Brush Up Co." At some point, the City also acquired an incongruous English overlay; some inhabitants speak with phony English accents, the Palace Guard wears "a costume that is a slightly exaggerated version of the English palace guards" (Langley, 93–94), and everyone sings a song in which the Emerald City is a "Jolly old town!" in "the Merry Old Land of Oz" (90–91).

Unlike Baum's Emerald City, the MGM City is genuinely green, outside and in—the only use of Baum's color theming in the film. Since in the original story the green color was an instance of false magic, the movie seems to suggest that its Emerald City is truly magical. The Horse of a Different Color—one of the film's most delightful inventions and wholly in the spirit of Baum—is real magic, and the "Wash & Brush Up Co." claims that it can dye Dorothy's eyes to match her gown. The Wizard's magic, however, is still a sham, and the scene of his unmasking—which the film combines with his presentation of pseudomagical gifts to the Scarecrow, the Woodman, and the Lion—is positioned as the climax of the entire film.

Providing yet another perspective on the significance of the Emerald City, the chorus of Optimistic Voices directs the travelers to

> Step into the sun
> Step into the light
> Keep straight ahead for
> The most glor ...
> ... ious place
> On the face
> Of the earth or the sky.
> (Langley, 86)

Here the City is unequivocally "glorious"; its association with light and the sun, combined with heavenly voices, suggests that it symbolizes a wholly positive, perhaps even spiritual state of being. In a slightly earlier version of the screenplay, this song was only part of a longer number entitled "The Land of Oz"; as Dorothy and her friends entered the City, they were to be greeted in person by the chorus, singing,

> Behold! You are in the Em'rald City of Oz
> We're told that a more enchanted land never was
> Behold your dream as it gleams in the sun
> Every beam is a jewel that shines for a deed well done
> Look high! There's a magic Make-Believe in the air
> And oh! If you still can use a dream … Take your share!
> A more enthralling vision of a wish-come-true never was
> So here's to the hearts that believe and belong
> In the land of Oz.
>
> (87)

The song not only urges the travelers (and the audience) to believe in the dreams and wishes clearly represented by the City, but makes them the reward of "deeds well done." It sends a clear and positive message about what the City stands for, but it was omitted from the final version of the screenplay. On balance, the Emerald City sequences leave us uncertain whether to believe wholeheartedly in the City, as we would like to do, or to dismiss it as a pleasant but unhelpful imposture, like the Wizard himself.[6]

The Witch's Castle and its surrounding landscape, on the other hand, express their significance with perfect clarity. As Glinda puts it, "Only bad witches are ugly" (Langley, 52), and the Wicked Witch inhabits an environment as dark, mean, and ugly as herself. The film does not show Dorothy and her friends leaving the City or their journey but jumps (rather too abruptly) from the corridor outside the Wizard's throne room to "a very creepy-looking wood" (102) only a mile from the Witch's Castle. This, as a sign informs us, is the "HAUNTED FOREST." It is night—an autumn night, apparently, for brown leaves litter the ground, and the scraggly, tangled trees are nearly bare. Black owls and crows, obviously fake, perch in the branches, blinking their red eyes. The comic, only mildly scary atmosphere of this scene may have been meant to reassure children who were about to be really frightened by the Flying Monkeys and the prisonlike interior of the Witch's Tower Room, where Dorothy would soon await her death. The Castle, a dark stone fortress, is perched on a rocky mountain high above the forest—at one point, the background music becomes, appropriately, Mussorgsky's "Night on a Bare Mountain"—in a landscape of barren crags shaped like Witch's hats. Far below, a river winds through a valley of cracked and lifeless rock. The sky is perpetually overcast; nearly the only thing that is not some shade of black or gray is the Witch's bright green skin.

To design the Haunted Forest and the Witch's Castle, Gibbons and Horning had no need for detailed descriptions. They could and did fall back on conventional images and associations. The moonlit Haunted Forest, with its hooting owls and talk of "spooks" and witches, conjures up the cluster of images associated with Halloween; the four travelers could almost be nervous trick-or-treaters in funny costumes. (Thus, the season here must be autumn, even though it is summer back in Munchkinland.) The Witch's Castle is a conventional medieval castle with a drawbridge, an entrance hall, towers, and battlements all specified by the screenplay. Gibbons and Horning kept its forms square and simple to create the look of a massive and impregnable fortress—one that could be successfully assailed only by the kind of trickery used by Dorothy's friends.

Like the Kansas landscape, the Witch's territory is set in opposition to the fertile, colorful, gently rounded landscape of Munchkinland. Both share the same oppressive gray sky. Yet they represent somewhat different states of being. Whereas the flat barrenness of Kansas suggests a condition of mental and emotional depression, the savage barrenness of the Witch's landscape—its jagged crags jutting aggressively into the sky—suggests active resentment and hatred. The leafless trees of the Haunted Forest, the naked mountains, even the bare stone walls and floors of her Castle express her hostility toward life itself. The tangle of crooked trees and the cobwebs hanging from the ceiling of the Tower Room also suggest the Witch's hatred of order—at least the kind of benign order represented by the harmless, picturesque ceremonies of Munchkinland. There is more than a hint of military dictatorship in the regimentation of her joylessly goose-stepping Winkies and bomberlike fleet of Flying Monkeys, reminding us that the militarization of Germany was very much in the news when the final version of the screenplay was written.[7]

It is in the events following the travelers' departure from the Emerald City that the plot of the movie begins to diverge most widely from that of the book—a divergence echoed by the entirely different landscapes described in each. Baum's Winkie Country, where the Witch rules, is a treeless, grassy plain that grows gradually rougher and hillier; near the Witch's Yellow Castle are great fields of butter-cups and yellow daisies (*Wizard*, 88). The nature of this landscape— wilder than the Munchkin country yet not hostile, and adorned with flowers—implies that it was not created by the Witch but usurped by her. Baum emphasizes, too, that the Winkies cannot be blamed when they attack the travelers; they are not free agents but the Witch's slaves, who "had to do as they were told." When they return defeated, the Witch "beat them well with a strap" (77). Baum's Flying Monkeys are not inherently wicked either; they must obey whoever wears the Golden Cap, and when Dorothy takes charge of the Cap, they become her servants.

In the film, on the other hand, the Winkies are much more men-acing. The screenplay describes them as "enormous" with "wicked-looking" weapons (Langley, 111); their tall fur hats make them look even taller, and as they march, they chant in sinister deep voices. The vocal arranger, Ken Darby, used a special recording technique that " 'made them sound like monsters' " (Harmetz, 98). Seen closer, moreover, they have green skin and long, pointed noses like the Witch's—indisputable evidence that the Witch herself is a Winkie rather than the alien usurper portrayed by Baum. True, once the Witch has been destroyed, the Winkies drop to their knees before Dorothy, exclaiming, "Hail to Dorothy! The Wicked Witch is dead!" (Langley, 119), but the suggestion that these Winkies, too, were unwilling slaves is passed over very quickly. As for the Winged Monkeys, they are wholly evil; Nikko, their leader, is described in the screenplay as the Witch's familiar (81). "I hate the Monkeys!" 14-year-old Ingrid John-son told me, as she recalled her memories of the film.[8]

In the book, Dorothy is never under real threat of death from the Witch; as Baum reminds us, she is protected by the magic of the Good Witch's kiss. In the film, Dorothy has no such protection, and the threat is both repeated and agonizingly prolonged. First Toto is to be drowned, a prospect nearly as upsetting to a child as the danger to Dorothy herself. Then the Witch realizes that the slippers will not come off till Dorothy is dead; sadistically toying with her victim, she leaves Dorothy with the running hourglass, telling her, "That's how much longer you've got to be alive" (Langley, 108). Alone in the Tower Room, with the camera turning periodically to the hourglass, Dorothy cries again and again, "I'm frightened, Auntie Em, I'm frightened!" (109). Aunt Em's face appears in the Witch's crystal ball, but she cannot see Dorothy, and her face dissolves into the mocking face of the Witch. Even after Dorothy's friends rescue her from the Tower Room, they are hunted down and trapped by the Winkie soldiers, and this time all four—five, counting Toto—are to be killed. One appreciates how many heartaches and nightmares Baum conscientiously avoided when one sees how determined the MGM screenwriters were to put them in.

Overall, the result is a picture of Oz several shades darker than the original. The absence of several of Baum's monsters from the film is more than compensated for by the more dominating presence of the Witch; it is hard to believe that she is on screen for only 12 minutes altogether (Harmetz, 296).[9] Unlike Baum's animal Kalidahs (who act merely by instinct) or the uncouth Hammer-Heads (who are not really dangerous), the Witch is a figure of conscious, implacable malevolence who has succeeded in creating a large part of Oz in her own image and nearly succeeds in killing Dorothy as well. Even the Wizard is initially presented in a way that some children find nearly as frightening as the Witch. Of the four different guises assumed by the Wizard in the book, the moviemakers combined the disembodied head and the ball of fire into one terrifying apparition; the revelation, several scenes later, of the harmless little man behind the curtain does not erase the powerful first impression of fiery monstrosity. The balance between good and evil elements in Oz, which in Baum's original tilted firmly toward the good, is at best an even one in the MGM film. Despite Dorothy's yearning for the world over the rainbow, she has scarcely arrived before she is fearfully telling Glinda, "Oh, I'd give anything to get out of Oz altogether" (Langley, 62).

A corollary of the greater power of evil in the MGM Oz is the diminished power of Dorothy—though most critics of the film consider her an impressive heroine. Salman Rushdie, for example, calls the film a "rite of passage" in which "the weakness of grownups forces children to take control of their own destinies, and so, ironically, grow up themselves." In Oz, Dorothy "is never, ever treated as a child but as a heroine. She gains this status by accident, it's true; ... but, by her adventure's end, she has certainly grown to fill those shoes—or, rather, those ruby slippers" (93). Aljean Harmetz, similarly, sees the story as one in which a child proves herself equal to an adult: "The child is stronger than the Bad Mother and takes on some of the responsibilities of the Good Mother in her nurturing of the maimed or incomplete men she meets along the Yellow Brick Road" (299). Ethan Mordden calls Dorothy "an adventurer of emblematic moral weight" (120) and points out that although the movie seems to be teaching her to go home and accept her place in the community,

> while she's in Oz she learns anything but subservience. On the contrary, she defies the power structure when she kills the two witches and virtually deposes the humbug Wizard, liberates the underclass in the persons of the Munchkins and the Winkies, and apparently leaves behind her an enlightened oligarchy to be led by her rehabilitated comrades.[10]

It's true that Dorothy accomplishes all this in the film (as she does in the book), yet if one turns directly from the book to the film, MGM's Dorothy seems noticeably less mature and capable. During the cyclone she shows none of the calm good sense of Baum's Dorothy; here and throughout the film she cries, screams, and calls for "Auntie Em" much more frequently. She is given no opportunity in the film to look after herself or travel on her own. Although both Dorothys are justifiably afraid of the Witch—and the movie's Dorothy, admittedly, has more to fear—it is Baum's Dorothy who hurls the water at the Witch in a blaze of anger. The movie's Dorothy never once fights back, and has to be rescued by her friends instead of rescuing them. In the book, Dorothy is given a particularly strong role after the Witch's death, freeing and directing the Winkies and assuming the power of the Golden Cap; the film allows her to do none of these things. Finally, whereas Baum's Dorothy journeys to Glinda on her own initiative, the movie's Dorothy waits passively for Glinda to rescue her once again, and is forced to repeat the lesson she has learned, like a good little schoolchild, before she can go home—where no one will believe what she has to tell them.

Most critics—and nearly every child who sees the movie—agree that its worst mistake was to explain away Dorothy's adventures and Oz itself as a dream.[11] "As art," says Harmetz, "the movie is flawed by its sentimentality, by its cheerful insistence that 'east, west, home is best,' and by the decision to void Dorothy's experience by making it into a dream" (299). Rushdie sees the decision as "bad faith," adding that only the "general integrity" of The Wizard "enabled it to transcend this hoary, creaking cliche" (98). Initially, the idea came from Noel Langley, who wrote the first complete script for the movie; his inspiration was The Poor Little Rich Girl (1917), a silent film starring Mary Pickford in which the little girl's servants reappear, grotesquely disguised, in her nightmare. At the first script conference with coproducers Freed and LeRoy, Langley argued that "you cannot put fantastic people in strange places in front of an audience unless they have seen them as human beings first" (Harmetz, 34). Mervyn LeRoy had his own suggestion: Dorothy would be reading The Wizard of Oz in bed; when she fell asleep, the book would fall and hit her on the head, causing her to dream the story. With Arthur Freed's support, however, Langley's idea prevailed, and from that point onward no one seems to have questioned the basic decision to make Dorothy dream her adventures instead of really having them. The result, as Harmetz says, is to "void Dorothy's experience." And since her experience has already been reduced to the sentiment that "There's no place like home," it is as though her entire journey has essentially been a waste of time. Whatever the film may have suggested about the power of dreams and aspirations, the journey through life, or the discovery of one's own potential is effectively invalidated by this ending.

The producers and screenwriters believed that the audience would be unable to accept fantastic characters in an imaginary world except within the context of a dream. There were practical reasons for their lack of confidence. Although Walt Disney's Snow White and the Seven Dwarfs had been one of Hollywood's most successful pictures in 1937, two recent big-budget fantasies using live actors—*Alice in Wonderland* in 1933 and *A Midsummer Night's Dream* in 1935—had been box office failures. But it also seems that the moviemakers themselves could not manage to believe in Oz. Having Dorothy say three times "There's no place like home"—apparently Arthur Freed's idea (Harmetz, 51)—expresses more than her desire to be with those she loves; Dorothy is also being made to renounce the world over the rainbow. Back in Kansas, when she tries to tell people that Oz was "a real truly live place," they laugh at her; she can only give up and say, "There's no place like home!" once again (Langley, 131–32). Oz becomes "no place" in the end.

This insistence on the unreality of Oz is reflected in the way Oz itself is portrayed, from the first moments in Munchkinland. Whereas Baum used the techniques of fantasy to lend a sense of reality to his imaginary world, the moviemakers used shiny plastic flowers and stylized painted backdrops to ensure that the audience would not mistake fantasy for reality. But their version of Oz is worse than unreal; it is untrustworthy. The world that seemed so delightful at first turns out to be dominated by the Witch; apple trees slap your hands; the beautiful fields of poppies through which the four friends run, rejoicing, toward the Emerald City are laden with deadly poison. The movie's Oz is not—as Baum's was—an essentially benign world where a Wicked Witch can rule only as a usurper; indeed, Glinda seems its only effective force for good. The implicit message, then, is not simply that the realm of the imagination is unreal, but that it is dangerous; trusting your imagination will not only mislead you, but will ultimately lead you into the nightmare of the Witch's Tower. It is no wonder that the Emerald City chorus that encouraged Dorothy and the audience to believe in the vision of Oz was omitted from the final version of the screenplay.

Although it seems strangely contradictory for a fantasy film to advocate distrust of fantasy, a negative attitude toward fantasy and the imagination is deeply rooted in American culture. In her essay "Why Are Americans Afraid of Dragons?" Ursula K. LeGuin relates this fear to the Puritanism that pervades American society, as well as to "our work ethic, our profit-mindedness, and even our sexual mores."[12] She suggests that American men, in particular, "have learned to repress their imagination, to reject it as something childish or effeminate, unprofitable, and probably sinful" (41–42). Unconsciously, no doubt, this attitude seeped into the film, so that as it evolved, the MGM *Wizard* became less of a tribute to the power of imagination than a warning against it.

For Baum, imagination was something to be wholeheartedly encouraged in the young. Thus, his imaginary world is not only "real"; despite occasional villains and monsters, it is a beautiful and happy place that children have always wanted to return to and explore. In Baum's story, Dorothy's desire to get home is not based on an inexplicable preference for Kansas, and her ultimate return to Oz later in the series, bringing her aunt and uncle with her, seems the ideal solution. Baum's *Wizard* encourages children's imaginations in other ways as well. The absence of any moral at the end of the story leaves it open to whatever meanings one can find in it—none of which are invalidated by the dismissal of the story as a dream, as they are in the film. And Baum's Oz includes a far greater variety of strange creatures and places, which is so large an element in its imaginative appeal. The Kalidahs, the talking mice, the China Country, the Hammer-Heads, the Quadling Country—all were omitted from the film.

Baum's fatherly concern for his young audience made him more sensitive than the MGM studio to their wants, needs, and fears. Although he included some frightening episodes in *The Wizard,* he was careful to keep them within bounds, and since Dorothy herself never becomes frantic or hysterical, the young audience stays calm, too. His Witch is never allowed to torment and terrorize Dorothy as the Witch does in the film. At the sneak preview, some small children were so terrified by the Witch that they had to be taken outside (Langley, 25); although some of her more threatening speeches were edited out, what remains can and still does give children nightmares. Through his Dorothy, Baum also gives more positive support to children's self-confidence and their ventures into independence; not only is she less fearful and tearful than the MGM Dorothy, and allowed more opportunities for decisive action, but she is not made to recant her visions at the end. The tension in the MGM *Wizard* between Dorothy's strength and heroism and what happens to her in the last minutes of the film has disturbed many viewers—sometimes to the point of protest. Todd Gilman, who sees Dorothy's dream as her subconscious rebellion against adult authority, quotes "a T-shirt popular in queer culture" that reads, "Aunt Em: Hate You! Hate Kansas! Taking the Dog. Dorothy" (161).

A deep sympathy for children is needed to understand how they really feel and what they care about—things that they may be unable to articulate themselves. Margaret Hamilton describes how her six-year-old son saw *The Wizard of Oz* for the first time at another child's birthday party; naturally anxious about his reaction to her portrayal of the Witch, she asked him afterward, "How did you like the movie?" He was silent.

> Then he said, "What did you do with those men?" "What men?" I asked. "You know, Mom, those big, tall men in the sort of fur hats; what did you do with them?" "Oh, well, you know, they're all actors, just as your mom is an actress, and acting is just pretending, so when the end of the day came we all took off our costumes and makeup and came home to our children." Silence. Then he said, "But what did you do with them?" "Nothing, dear, they are not really guards; I am not really a witch, am I?" "No. But what did you do with them?" I was a little desperate; then I realized that I had not listened to his question. I was answering something that I had not been asked. "You see, the Witch had cast a spell on the guards," I explained, "and they had no choice; they had to do as she wished until she was melted.... Then her spell was broken and they were all free to do as they wished and I am sure they wished to go home." "Oh," he said with a sigh of evident relief. "I see." (Harmetz, xx)

Sometimes it's hard even for a mother to know what question a child is really asking, and the film, as we've seen, leaves the child's question unanswered. Nothing is shown or said of the Winkie guards after the melting of the Witch, except for that very brief exchange when they hail Dorothy and give her the broomstick. Sharp enough to guess that the guards had served the Witch involuntarily, and compassionate enough to feel concern for them, Margaret Hamilton's son was left wondering what had become of them after the Witch was gone. If it had occurred to any of the film's 10 screenwriters that a child might ask that question, no answer survived in the final version of the screenplay.

Baum, on the other hand, clarifies that the Winkies "were the slaves of the Wicked Witch and too afraid of her not to do as she told them" (*Wizard*, 81), encouraging his young readers to feel compassion for them. And far from leaving their fate uncertain, Baum describes in detail what freedom meant to them:

> There was great rejoicing among the yellow Winkies, for they had been made to work hard during many years for the Wicked Witch, who had always treated them with great cruelty. They kept this day as a holiday, then and ever after, and spent the time in feasting and dancing. (84)

Baum explains how the Winkies helped Dorothy restore the Tin Woodman and the Scarecrow to full health, how sorry the Winkies were to see them leave, and how they "had grown so fond of the Tin Woodman that they begged him to stay and rule over them, and the Yellow Land of the West" (87). He describes the keepsakes the Winkies gave the travelers—golden collars for Toto and the Lion, a diamond bracelet for Dorothy, a gold-headed walking stick for the Scarecrow, and for the Tin Woodman, "a silver oil-can, inlaid with gold and set with precious jewels." And at the end of the book, he tells how the Tin Woodman decides, with Glinda's approval, to accept the Winkies' offer. " 'I am sure,' " says Glinda, " 'that you will rule the Winkies wisely and well' "(130). It matters to Baum what happened to the Winkies, just as it matters to a child.

Though *The Wizard of Oz* is a classic children's film—exciting to watch, stimulating to the imagination, full of memorable scenes and characters, rich with meaning—children will find a better friend in L. Frank Baum.

# Appendix:
# Approaches to Teaching *The Wizard of Oz*

Baum's classic fantasy is an excellent choice for the classroom. It can be shared with a wide range of ages; while younger children absorb it chapter by chapter as a read-aloud, older ones can read its clear, unassuming prose for themselves. Its underlying themes are plain enough for eight-year-olds to identify and talk about, and older children and even teenagers will enjoy analyzing the techniques Baum uses to create his imaginary world and the differences between book and film versions. The story is free from the ethnic, racial, class, or gender biases that pose difficulties within many other children's classics; indeed, the value of diversity is something Baum emphasizes throughout the Oz books. And Dorothy is one of the few female characters whom boys have never hesitated to adopt as their protagonist. Her resolute spirit, her intelligence, her kindness and courtesy, her loyalty to family and friends—all make her a worthy yet never too obvious role model for boys and girls alike.

Through Dorothy, Baum encourages children to believe that they too could survive catastrophe, master a strange new environment, and find their own way home. His dominant theme is that we all possess inner resources of which we are unaware—resources ample to see us successfully through life's journey. Without teaching or preaching, no author does more than Baum to nourish a sense of confidence and self-worth in a child.

Stories of pure fantasy, such as the Oz books, are of course unsurpassed at stretching the child's ability to imagine, speculate, and dream—but Baum goes a step further. Like his great predecessor Lewis Carroll, Baum also stimulates children to become active rather than passive readers. He never tells them that the Scarecrow already has brains, that the Tin Woodman is already tenderhearted, and the Cowardly Lion already brave. Instead, he allows the characters to demonstrate intelligence, tenderness, and courage in so many and various situations that children can discover this themselves. When the four travelers are halted in their path by a deep ravine, for example, the intelligent Scarecrow is the one to suggest that the Lion can jump across it, carrying them one at a time, while the Lion's response demonstrates his courage.

> "Well, I'll try it," said the Lion. "Who will go first?"
>
> "I will," declared the Scarecrow; "for, if you found that you could not jump over the gulf, Dorothy would be killed, or the Tin Woodman badly dented on the rocks below. But if I am on your back it will not matter so much, for the fall would not hurt me at all."
>
> "I am terribly afraid of falling, myself," said the Cowardly Lion, "but I suppose there is nothing to do but try it. So get on my back and we will make the attempt." (*Wizard*, 92)

In episodes such as this, Baum not only reveals the inner truth about his characters but sets up situations designed for problem-solving. Given the physical characteristics of the Scarecrow, the Tin Woodman, and Dorothy, who should make the first jump with the Lion? Or again, which of the travelers will be immune to the soporific poppy fumes, and how can they rescue their unconscious friends? Baum clearly enjoys the kind of logical thinking needed to solve such problems, and he expects the young reader to enjoy it too.

Like Carroll, Baum includes other kinds of questions—problems less practical than philosophical, as in the famous debate between the Scarecrow and the Tin Woodman:

> "All the same," said the Scarecrow, "I shall ask for the brains instead of a heart; for a fool would not know what to do with a heart if he had one."

"I shall take the heart," returned the Tin Woodman; "For brains do not make one happy, and happiness is the best thing in the world." (*Wizard*, 84)

Dorothy, says Baum, "was puzzled to know which of her two friends was right," and he does not supply an answer but leaves the problem for young readers to puzzle over—just as Carroll had invited them to imagine what becomes of a candle flame when the candle is blown out.

Despite the simplicity of its style, *The Wizard* is rich in opportunities for young readers to practice active reading, and one cannot do better in teaching it than to follow Baum's lead. One might pause, for example, after reading aloud the Lion's " 'Who will go first?' " and ask listeners which character *should* go first, and why, before reading the Scarecrow's solution. Or students might be asked whether *they* would choose a heart or a brain. Other discussion topics can easily be adapted from earlier chapters in this book. Older children, as I have suggested, should find it interesting to analyze the techniques used by writers of fantasy, as described in chapter 6; they can try these techniques themselves by building imaginary worlds of their own. If a whole world seems too ambitious, they can create an imaginary country within the world of Oz, built like the China Country on a single premise, and write a new chapter in which Dorothy and her friends visit it.

Students often comment spontaneously on how different the book is from the MGM film, with which nearly all are familiar. Lively discussions can be generated from such issues as the sentimentalization of the "No place like home" theme in the film version and the film's suggestion that the whole adventure was a dream—or from the question of whether Baum himself would have approved of the film. Excerpts from Salman Rushdie's book might be used with older students. Another excellent resource is *The Making of "The Wizard of Oz"* by Aljean Harmetz, with its detailed "inside story" of the film. Older children are fascinated by the technology of special effects and will enjoy learning about the Tin Woodman's elaborate makeup, how the cyclone was created, and the time Margaret Hamilton caught on fire.

Comparing the illustrations of different artists for the same story is the perfect way to teach children the concept of interpretation. Younger children who hear the story read aloud can do their own illustrations and compare them with each other's. (It might be a good idea to choose scenes that don't appear in the movie.) Older children can compare different editions of *The Wizard,* analyzing and evaluating various illustrators' interpretations of scenes and characters. Many illustrated editions are available, including facsimiles of the original edition with W. W. Denslow's illustrations and editions illustrated by Barry Moser, Greg Hildebrandt, Evelyn Copelman, Maraja, Alan Atkinson, and Michael Hague.

*The Wizard* lends itself happily to activities in a number of subject areas. Mapmaking, for example, can incorporate math, geography, and art, and is fun besides. After learning how explorers like Lewis and Clark map a new territory, students can construct a map of Oz from the information provided in *The Wizard,* figuring out about how many miles Dorothy could walk each day so that they can draw their map to scale. When they've finished, they can compare their map to Professor Wogglebug's "official" map of Oz. Such an activity also encourages close and active reading.

Transforming a two-dimensional map into a relief map with miniature roads, forests, and castles is particularly enjoyable and again reinforces basic geographical concepts. Or the map could be expanded with a series of dioramas depicting different locations—the Munchkin village, the Witch's Castle, the land of the Hammer-Heads, or the Emerald City. Or it could become the basis for a board game. The process of inventing and playing such a game is again a natural way of combining elements from several subject areas, from art to mathematics. Because of its emphasis on color, the map of Oz could even introduce older students to the famous "four-color problem" in topology—the proposition that no map can be drawn that needs more than four colors to demarcate its territories.

The familiar map of North America may be used as well. By learning something of Baum's life story and then locating and marking on this map the places in which he lived—from New York state to the Midwest and finally to California—students can gain a sense not only of Baum's life and its relationship to the Oz books but of the great westward population shift of the late nineteenth century. Students might also learn about the Chicago Columbian Exposition of 1893, study pictures of the White City, and decide for themselves whether it may have inspired the Emerald City of Oz.

Some of the most spectacular events in *The Wizard* are based on science rather than magic and provide a jumping-off point for science activities and investigations. The cyclone that carries Dorothy to Oz can introduce students to real-life cyclones and hurricanes. Balloons also play a major role in the story; the Wizard constructs a balloon to fly himself and Dorothy home from Oz, and Baum includes a simple explanation of how gas and hot-air balloons work. Students can try a hot-air balloon experiment of their own, using paper bags. They can learn about the first balloon flights, watch a video of a hot-air balloon trip, and enjoy Mary Calhoun's *Hot-Air Henry* (for younger children) or William Pène du Bois's Newbery Award winner *The Twenty-One Balloons* (for older children).

While reading about Dorothy's visit to the Emerald City, it's fun to wear glasses with green lenses, like those designed by the Wizard for its inhabitants. These are easy to make with a little thin cardboard, pipe cleaners, and green cellophane paper. A more ambitious craft project would be a full-sized scarecrow stuffed with straw, following Baum's detailed description.

To broaden their knowledge of Oz, a class might join the International Wizard of Oz Club, which sponsors an Oz Pen Pal Association and *The Oz Gazette,* to which young people contribute their own letters, articles, puzzles, and artwork. Or they could explore any of several Oz discussion groups on the Internet.

Celebrating the birthdays of authors and illustrators is always a welcome excuse for promoting children's books. Baum's birthday is May 15. (An alternative date would be May 6. This, according to the film of *The Wizard,* is the date of Dorothy's arrival in Oz, as indicated on the death certificate of the Wicked Witch of the East. It was also the date of Baum's own death.) In advance of the celebration, students might do some research on Baum's life, mark the places he lived on a map, and decorate the room with their own illustrations, the map of

Oz, and flags bearing the colors of Oz and its regions. Party-goers could wear green glasses, eat green-frosted cake, and drink green lemonade. (In the Emerald City, Baum tells us, "[A] man was selling green lemonade, and when the children bought it Dorothy could see that they paid for it with green pennies" [*Wizard,* 117].) Or students might dress up as Munchkins in blue jeans and blue Munchkin hats, sing "We're Off to See the Wizard," and read aloud or act out a favorite episode. Students can then begin a new Oz book; *Ozma of Oz,* in which Dorothy first returns to Oz, would be a good choice.

*The Wizard of Oz* can lead naturally to other books in the series—or it can be the starting point for an entire literature-based curriculum unit on the theme of imaginary worlds. A class of third-graders could visit three or four imaginary worlds: Oz, the country of the elephants in Jean de Brunhoff's Babar books, Maurice Sendak's land *Where the Wild Things Are,* and Wild Island in Ruth Stiles Gannett's *My Father's Dragon.* Older children could explore more worlds, reading some books in groups or on their own. Some outstanding works of fantasy featuring imaginary worlds include

*Through the Looking-Glass* by Lewis Carroll
*The Hobbit* by J. R. R. Tolkien
*The Lion, the Witch and the Wardrobe* and other Chronicles of Narnia
  by C. S. Lewis
*Finn Family Moomintroll* and other tales of Moominland by Tove Jansson
*The Book of Three* and other Chronicles of Prydain by Lloyd Alexander
*The Gammage Cup* and *The Firelings* by Carol Kendall
*Cart and Cwidder* by Diana Wynne Jones
*Dinotopia* and *The World Beneath* by James Gurney
*The Magic City* by E. Nesbit.

The most advanced readers might enjoy Ursula K. LeGuin's *Wizard of Earthsea,* Robin McKinley's *Blue Sword* and *The Hero and the Crown,* Poul Anderson's *Three Hearts and Three Lions,* or J. R. R. Tolkien's *Lord of the Rings.*

"Imaginary worlds" could include other planets, widening the scope of the unit to include science fiction. Eleanor Cameron's *Won-*

*derful Flight to the Mushroom Planet* is a delightful introduction to interplanetary travel for seven- or eight-year-olds. Older children might visit John Christopher's Moon (in *The Lotus Caves*), Robert A. Heinlein's Mars (in *Red Planet*), H. M. Hoover's Eridan (in *The Rains of Eridan*), or William Sleator's world of the fifth dimension in *The Boy Who Reversed Himself.*

Poetry should be included in this rich mixture: Edward Lear's "Owl and the Pussycat" or "The Jumblies"; Walter de la Mare's "Tartary," "Suppose," or "Under the Rose"; Tennyson's "Blow, Bugle, Blow"; Denise Levertov's "Psalm Concerning the Castle"; or Coleridge's "Kubla Khan." One might give older students a taste of Thomas More's *Utopia;* Shakespeare's *Tempest; Gulliver's Travels;* Plato's Atlantis; or Charlotte Perkins Gilman's feminist utopia *Herland.* And the great artists who have depicted imaginary worlds range from Renaissance painters such as Brueghel and Mantegna, to nineteenth-century visionaries such as Thomas Cole and the Pre-Raphaelites, to the surrealists of our own century.

The theme of imaginary worlds can lead to thought-provoking discussions for students at any age level. For example, what is a utopia? What utopian elements can we find in these worlds? What utopian elements might you want to include in your own imaginary world? Which of these worlds seem to be created to test or educate the characters, and what is the nature of the test or education that each provides?

Many of the activities I've suggested for *The Wizard,* such as making maps, designing games, and creating dioramas—could be expanded to take in other worlds. Students could be assigned in small groups to read different books and report on their worlds to the rest of the class. They might also enjoy writing up their worlds in the form of guidebooks. After studying some sample tourist guides to real-life countries, students can adopt the tone and style of these guides while describing, for example, the main tourist attractions, flora, fauna, customs, food, lodging, souvenirs, and transportation systems of an imaginary world. Compiling and writing such a guide demands not only close and active reading of the original text but a wide range of writing skills—from organizing masses of detail to tailoring one's prose to a specific audience and purpose. At the culmination of this curriculum unit, the guidebooks, maps, and artwork depicting imaginary worlds would make a wonderful display.

The possibilities are as limitless as the worlds themselves.

# Notes and References

## Chapter 1

1. Frank Joslyn Baum and Russell P. MacFall, *To Please a Child: A Biography of L. Frank Baum, Royal Historian of Oz* (Chicago: Reilly and Lee, 1961); hereafter cited in text.

2. For the history of American fantasy before Baum, see Brian Attebery, *The Fantasy Tradition in American Literature: From Irving to Le Guin* (Bloomington: Indiana University Press, 1980); hereafter cited in text. Mark West's *Before Oz: Juvenile Fantasy Stories from Nineteenth-Century America* (Hamden, Conn.: Archon Books, 1989) includes a representative sampling of pre-Baum American fantasy for children.

## Chapter 2

1. L. Frank Baum, *The Wizard of Oz*, Critical Heritage Series, ed. Michael Patrick Hearn (New York: Schocken, 1983), 2; hereafter cited in text as *Wizard*.

2. Allen Eyles, *The World of Oz* (Tucson: HP Books, 1985), 9. Angelica Shirley Carpenter and Jean Shirley, *L. Frank Baum: Royal Historian of Oz* (Minneapolis: Lerner, 1992), 129; hereafter cited in text.

3. A story by Charles Savage entitled "The Dark Side of the Rainbow," published 1 August 1995 in the *Fort Wayne Journal Gazette* and later widely circulated on the Internet, claims that a synchronous relationship exists between the MGM *Wizard* and the Pink Floyd album *The Dark Side of the Moon;* playing the album simultaneously with the film results in numerous matches between the music and lyrics of the songs and the action of the film.

4. For a full account of the auction, see Aljean Harmetz, *The Making of "The Wizard of Oz": Movie Magic and Studio Power in the Prime of MGM—and the Miracle of Production #1060* (New York: Alfred A. Knopf, 1977), 303–9; hereafter cited in text.

# Chapter 3

1. Michael Patrick Hearn, *The Annotated Wizard of Oz* (New York: Clarkson N. Potter, 1973), 36–37; hereafter cited in text as Hearn 1973. Hearn gives a complete account of Baum's partnership with Denslow and what led to its dissolution.

2. See Hearn's comments in *The Annotated Wizard of Oz*, 67–68.

3. Michael Patrick Hearn, ed., *The Wizard of Oz*, by L. Frank Baum, Critical Heritage Series (New York: Schocken, 1983), 147; hereafter cited in text as Hearn 1983.

4. Gore Vidal comments in "On Rereading the Oz Books," "To the extent that Baum makes his readers aware that our country's 'practical' arrangements are inferior to those of Oz, he is a truly subversive writer and it is no wonder that the Librarian of Detroit finds him cowardly and negative, because, of course, he is brave and affirmative" (Hearn 1983, 270).

5. For an account of a recent attempt from the religious right wing to censor the Oz books, see Carpenter and Shirley, 134.

6. James Thurber's essay, as well as those by Paul Gallico, Gore Vidal, Martin Gardner, Ray Bradbury, Russel B. Nye, and C. Warren Hollister can be found in Hearn 1983.

7. Martin Gardner and Russel B. Nye, *The Wizard of Oz and Who He Was* (East Lansing, Mich.: Michigan State University Press, 1957); hereafter cited in text.

8. Zena Sutherland and May Hill Arbuthnot, *Children and Books* (New York: HarperCollins, 1991), 279.

9. Cornelia Meigs et al., *A Critical History of Children's Literature* (New York: Macmillan, 1969), 412.

10. Humphrey Carpenter and Mari Prichard, *The Oxford Companion to Children's Literature* (Oxford: Oxford University Press, 1984), 51.

11. John Rowe Townsend, *Written for Children: An Outline of English-Language Children's Literature*, 4th ed. (New York: HarperCollins, 1992), 83–84.

12. Martin Gardner, "Why Librarians Dislike Oz," in Hearn 1983, 187–91.

13. For an analysis of the commercial aspect of Oz, see Richard Flynn, "Imitation Oz: The Sequel as Commodity," *Lion and the Unicorn* 20 (1996): 121–31.

14. Marius Bewley, "The Land of Oz: America's Great Good Place," in Hearn 1983, 199–207; hereafter cited in text.

15. Jordan Brotman, "A Late Wanderer in Oz," *Chicago Review* 18 (1965): 63–73.

16. Henry M. Littlefield, "The Wizard of Oz: Parable on Populism," in Hearn 1983, 221–33; hereafter cited in text. It should be noted that Littlefield himself repudiated this interpretation in "The Wizard of Allegory," *Baum Bugle* 36 (Spring 1992). According to his own account, it was the result of an exercise assigned to a high school history class.

17. Fred Erisman, "L. Frank Baum and the Progressive Dilemma," *American Quarterly* 20 (Fall 1968): 616–23.

18. Stuart Culver, "What Manikins Want: *The Wonderful Wizard of Oz* and *The Art of Decorating Dry Goods Windows*," *Representations* 21 (Winter 1988): 97–116.

19. William Leach, *Land of Desire: Merchants, Power, and the Rise of a New American Culture* (New York: Pantheon, 1993), 251; hereafter cited in text.

20. S. J. Sackett, "The Utopia of Oz," in Hearn 1983, 207–21; hereafter cited in text.

21. Jack Zipes, *Fairy Tales and the Art of Subversion: The Classical Genre for Children and the Process of Civilization* (New York: Methuen, 1983), 101.

22. Jack Zipes, *Fairy Tale as Myth/Myth as Fairy Tale* (Lexington: University Press of Kentucky, 1994), 119.

23. Noah Seaman and Barbara Seaman, "Munchkins, Ozophiles, and Feminists Too," *Ms.*, January 1974, 93.

24. Joel D. Chaston, "If I Ever Go Looking for My Heart's Desire: 'Home' in Baum's 'Oz' Books," *Lion and the Unicorn* 18 (December 1994): 209–19.

25. Sheldon Kopp, "The Wizard of Oz behind the Couch," *Psychology Today* 3 (March 1970): 70.

26. Osmond Beckwith, "The Oddness of Oz," in Hearn 1983, 233–47.

27. J. Karl Franson, "From Vanity Fair to Emerald City: Baum's Debt to Bunyan," *Children's Literature* 23 (1995): 91–114.

28. Paul Nathanson, *Over the Rainbow: "The Wizard of Oz" as a Secular Myth of America* (New York: State University of New York, 1991).

# Chapter 4

1. L. Frank Baum, "Modern Fairy Tales," in Hearn 1983, 139.

2. I am indebted for this suggestion to my student Violet Simmons.

3. Quoted in Suzanne Rahn, *Rediscoveries in Children's Literature* (New York: Garland, 1995), 5.

4. An analysis of Tik-Tok as an early example of a true robot and a possible influence on Isaac Asimov's robots and their Three Laws can be

found in "Tik-Tok and the Three Laws of Robotics," by Paul M. Abrahm and Stuart Kenter, in *Science-Fiction Studies 5* (March 1978): 67–80.

5. Frank Stockton, *The Floating Prince and Other Fairy Tales* (New York: Scribners, 1881), 2.

6. Edward Bellamy, *Looking Backward, 2000–1887* (Mattituck, N.Y.: American Reprint, n.d.), 83–84.

7. L. Frank Baum, *The Emerald City of Oz* (Chicago: Reilly and Britton, 1910), 30–31; hereafter cited in text as *Emerald*.

8. Quoted in Marshall B. Davidson, *The American Heritage History of the Writers' America* (New York: American Heritage Publishing, 1973), 269.

9. Baum explains fully in *The Tin Woodman of Oz* (Chicago: Reilly and Britton, 1918): After Oz was enchanted by the fairy Queen Lurline,

> From that moment no one in Oz ever died. Those who were old, remained old; those who were young and strong did not change as the years passed by; the children remained children always, and played and romped to their hearts' content, while all the babies lived in their cradles and were tenderly cared for and never grew up. So people of Oz stopped counting how old they were in years, for years made no difference in their appearance and could not alter their station. They did not get sick, so there were no doctors among them. Accidents might happen to some, on rare occasions, it is true, and while no one could die naturally as other people do, it was possible that one might be totally destroyed. Such incidents, however, were very unusual, and so seldom was there anything to worry over that the people of Oz were as happy and contented as could be. (156–57)

10. William Morris, *Selected Writings and Designs* (Harmondsworth, Eng.: Penguin, 1962), 188; hereafter cited in text.

11. L. Frank Baum, *The Patchwork Girl of Oz* (Chicago: Reilly and Britton, 1913), 181; hereafter cited in text as *Patchwork*.

12. L. Frank Baum, *The Road to Oz* (Chicago: Reilly and Britton, 1909), 189; hereafter cited in text.

13. A question often used to discredit peaceful utopias is whether utopian principles could survive in the face of a hostile invasion from a nonutopian country. Does the utopia jettison its ideals and go to war, or does it allow itself to be conquered? In either case, it would no longer be a utopia. In *The Emerald City of Oz*, Baum deals with this difficult question as well. The Nome King gathers an army to conquer Oz, but the firmly pacifist Ozma, through her intelligent use of magic, is able to save her country without resort to bloodshed.

14. Quoted in "Oz under Scrutiny: Early Reviews of the Marvelous Land of Oz," *Baum Bugle* 23 (Spring 1979): 14.

15. *A Week at the Fair, Illustrating the Exhibits and Wonders of the World's Columbian Exposition* (Chicago: Rand McNally, 1893), 32; hereafter cited in text as *Week*.

16. Ben C. Truman, *History of the World's Fair: Being a Complete Description of the World's Columbian Exposition from Its Inception* (Chicago: Waverly, 1893), 448; hereafter cited in text.

17. The entire text of Mrs. Potter Palmer's speech, along with the enthusiastic reactions of her audience, can be found in Major Ben Truman's *History of the World's Fair*. The Board of Lady Managers was also responsible for the Children's Building nearby, a kind of day care center where mothers could safely leave young children while they toured the fair.

18. Baum was not fond, however, of aggressively militant feminists—like his mother-in-law, perhaps?—and good-humoredly satirized them in *The Land of Oz* (1904).

19. L. Frank Baum, *The Magic of Oz* (Chicago: Reilly and Lee, 1919), 54; hereafter cited in text as *Magic*.

20. Arnold Berke, "The White City and Our Cities," *Historic Preservation News* 33 (February 1993): 6.

# Chapter 5

1. *A New Wonderland* (New York: R. H. Russell, 1900) was later republished as *The Surprising Adventures of the Magical Monarch of Mo* (Indianapolis: Bobbs-Merrill, 1903); the title was shortened in subsequent editions to *The Magical Monarch of Mo*.

2. For discussion and some alternative theories on the origin of the name "Oz," see Hearn's *Annotated Wizard of Oz*, 103, and Gardner and Nye's *Wizard of Oz and Who He Was*, 37–38.

3. " 'Dear Sergeant Snow': Maud Gage Baum's Correspondence with Jack Snow," *Baum Bugle* 26 (Winter 1982): 10.

4. Dorothy's last name is first mentioned in the 1902 stage musical of *The Wizard of Oz* and is first used in the Oz books in *Ozma of Oz* (Hearn 1973, 107).

5. Wagner, the biographer of Baum's mother-in-law, had learned of the tombstone from Dorothy's surviving sister, Matilda Jewell Gage. "Real Dorothy's Tombstone Discovered," in "Oz and Ends," *Baum Bugle* 40 (Winter 1996): 5; hereafter cited in text as "Real."

6. Although *The Wizard* ends with the Silver Shoes lost in the desert, subsequent volumes place Dorothy in possession of an equally impres-

sive source of power, the Magic Belt. As Gore Vidal puts it, "Dorothy's will to power is a continuing force in the series" (Hearn 1983, 264).

7. C.S. Lewis, "On Three Ways of Writing for Children," in *Of Other Worlds: Essays and Stories* (New York: Harcourt Brace and World, 1966), 33.

8. Robert Holdstock and Malcolm Edwards, *Alien Landscapes* (New York: Mayflower, 1979).

9. Gaston Bachelard, *The Poetics of Space* (*La poetique de l'espace*), trans. Maria Jolas (Boston: Beacon Press, 1969), xxxii.

10. Martin Gardner comments on this episode: "Dorothy may still have this key. It would be interesting to know if the old farm house is still standing at the spot where the cyclone left it" (Gardner and Nye, 197).

# Chapter 6

1. Katy Lau, "An Ozzy 'Aloha' from a Hawaiian Fan," *Oz Gazette* 8 (Winter 1996):, 1; hereafter cited in text.

2. In a personal conversation on 17 May 1997.

3. Sarah Hayes, "Fan Dreams of Life in Oz," *Oz Gazette* 9 (Spring 1997): 1.

4. The current address of the International Wizard of Oz Club is The International Wizard of Oz Club, Inc., P.O. Box 266, Kalamazoo, Michigan 49004-0266.

5. Lili Peller, "Daydreams and Children's Favorite Books," *Psychoanalytic Study of the Child* 14 (1959): 431.

6. Lewis Carroll, *The Annotated Alice: "Alice's Adventures in Wonderland" and "Through the Looking-Glass,"* ed. Martin Gardner (New York: Bramhall House, 1960), 25–26.

7. George MacDonald, "The Fantastic Imagination," in *A Peculiar Gift: Nineteenth Century Writings on Books for Children,* ed. Lance Salway (Harmondsworth, Eng.: Penguin, 1976), 162–63; hereafter cited in text.

8. Hugh Pendexter, "Magic in Thompson's Oz," *Baum Bugle* 22 (Autumn 1978): 2; hereafter cited in text.

9. Some well-known examples from science fiction depicting worlds in which scientific magic takes the place of science include Robert A. Heinlein's *Magic, Inc.;* Poul Anderson's *Operation Chaos;* L. Sprague de Camp and Fletcher Pratt's *The Incomplete Enchanter;* and Randall Garrett's *Too Many Magicians* and others in the Lord Darcy series. A notable example from fantasy is Ursula K. Le Guin's *Wizard of Earthsea,* with its school for wizards.

10. Hugh Pendexter distinguishes between "magical technology, in which magic tools and devices imitate the advances of the outside world, and

magical talismans which have powers in no way connected with the normal functioning of the object" (6). Both types of magical objects occur in Oz. Tik-Tok, the mechanical man, would be an example of magical technology and the Golden Cap an example of a magical talisman.

11. L. Frank Baum, *The Life and Adventures of Santa Claus* (1902; reprint, New York: Exposition Press, 1971), 117.

12. "On the Liquidation of Witches," by Dr. Douglas A. Rossman (*Baum Bugle*, Spring 1969), suggests a scientific explanation for the destruction of both witches. Michael Patrick Hearn summarizes Rossman's argument:

> Adhesion, the sticking together of molecules in contact with each other, may be broken down either by water or by another powerful force, such as a strong blow. The Witch cannot bleed because her bodily liquids dried up years before; with the loss of natural liquids the ability of adhesion to combat other forces is lessened. Only her black arts have kept her from literally falling apart. When water is poured on this dry substance, the adhesion is disrupted and the molecular structure falls apart. When Dorothy's house falls upon the Wicked Witch of the East, the impact of the blow is so great that this also breaks down the molecular structure, and she falls apart into dust. (1973, 234)

13. As Hearn notes in *The Annotated Wizard of Oz,* "Baum's use of white as the witch color is another reversal of the generally accepted ways of the world" (115). However, he sidesteps the question of whether even wicked witches wear white by never describing the clothing of the Wicked Witches of the East and West. The MGM movie abandoned Baum's innovation, dressing the Wicked Witch of the West entirely in black and Glinda in frilly pink—and creating a further distinction based (unfortunately) on looks: "Only bad witches are ugly!" Glinda says sweetly.

14. Post-Baum examples of fantasies with accompanying maps include *Winnie-the-Pooh* by A. A. Milne, the Prydain series by Lloyd Alexander, the Moomintroll series by Tove Jansson, *Watership Down* by Richard Adams, *A Wizard of Earthsea* by Ursula K. Le Guin, *The Gammage Cup* and *The Firelings* by Carol Kendall, *My Father's Dragon* by Ruth Stiles Gannett, and *Mistress Masham's Repose* by T. H. White. Two excellent sources for maps of imaginary worlds are J. B. Post, *An Atlas of Fantasy* (Baltimore: Mirage, 1973), which includes distant planets from science fiction, and Alberto Manguel and Gianni Guadalupi, *The Dictionary of Imaginary Places* (New York: Macmillan, 1980), which does not include other planets.

15. These maps, which can be purchased at a low price from the International Wizard of Oz Club, are indispensable for anyone who wishes to explore the geography of Baum's imaginary world; locations from Ruth

Plumly Thompson's Oz books are included as well. An (anonymous) article on "The Maps of Oz," which includes five alternative versions with comments from the cartographers, can be found in *The Best of the Baum Bugle, 1963–1964,* ed. Bugle Editors (Kinderhook, Ill.: International Wizard of Oz Club, 1975).

16.   Baum also designed colored flags for Oz; while each country, as one would expect, flies a flag of its own color, the banner of Ozma duplicates the map of Oz—a green center surrounded by four quarters colored blue, purple, yellow, and red, "indicating that she rules over all the countries of the Land of Oz" (*Magic,* 55). For a more detailed analysis of the color geography of Oz and the theory underlying it, see Hearn 1973, 114–15.

17.   For a discussion of Baum's religious and Theosophical beliefs, see Hearn 1973, 69–73. Baum's connection to Theosophy is discussed less sympathetically in William Leach's *Land of Desire,* 246–59.

18.   *Entertainments for All Seasons* (New York: S. H. Moore, 1904). For example, the chapter on how to give a Lemon Party begins,

> For a lemon party the hostess sends her invitations out on yellow paper, also requesting each guest to bring a lemon. Then she hunts up yellow lanterns for lawn and porch, and hangs her rooms in yellow crepe and yellow flower garlands. Her lamp and candle shades are yellow crepe paper, and yellow jardinieres with clusters of yellow flowers stand here and there. The lady herself must be decked in a lovely yellow gown, to fit the occasion. (163)

The refreshments include chicken salad served in lemon shells, lemonade, and lemon cake. "When the guests depart, give each one a little yellow box filled with lemon drops, as a parting pleasantry" (164).

19.   In 1957, Walt Disney announced a feature film using live actors, including many of the Mouseketeers, to be entitled *The Rainbow Road to Oz,* but the project went no further than a few musical numbers, which were presented on the television show *Disneyland* on 11 September 1957. For a full account, see David R. Smith, "Walt Disney and the Rainbow Road to Oz," *Baum Bugle* 24 (Winter 1980–1981): 2–7.

20.   See especially William Leach, *Land of Desire,* 253–55. "He is a confidence man," Leach writes of the Wizard, "a cheat, a deceptive swami, a conniving display illusionist. But what is the response to his behavior? Outrage? Fury? No—surprisingly, no one really cares" (253–54). Leach's argument that the Oz books encouraged the development of American consumer culture is weakened by such distortions as his insistence that the Wizard is "the leading character" (253) of *The Wizard* and such omissions as the economic system described in *The Emerald City* (which is clearly not capitalism).

21.  See Beth Dunlop, *Building a Dream: The Art of Disney Architecture* (New York: Harry N. Abrams, 1996). Disneyland's Main Street, to give only one example, is thought to have been a source of inspiration both for pedestrian malls and for the Historic Preservation movement. Brian Attebery comments on the resemblance between the White City and Disneyland in "Theme Parks and Urban Growth," *Para.Doxa* 2.1 (1996): 6–9.

22.  Ray Bradbury, "Because, Because, Because, Because of the Wonderful Things He Does," in Hearn 1983, 249.

23.  William Lindsay Gresham, "The Scarecrow to the Rescue," *Baum Bugle* 39 (Autumn 1995): 21.

## Chapter 7

1.  A thorough account of the entire production process is provided in Aljean Harmetz, *The Making of "The Wizard of Oz."* The evolution of the screenplay is also described in Michael Patrick Hearn's introduction to Noel Langley, Florence Ryerson, and Edgar Allen Woolf, *The Wizard of Oz: The Screenplay* (New York: Dell, 1989); hereafter cited in text as "Langley."

2.  For an analysis of the contradictions in Baum's Oz films, see Anne Morey, " 'A Whole Book for a Nickel'? L. Frank Baum as Filmmaker" in *Children's Literature Association Quarterly* 20 (Winter 1995–1996): 155–60.

3.  The music playing in the background, with heavy-handed irony, is Robert Schumann's "The Happy Farmer."

4.  Salman Rushdie, *The Wizard of Oz,* BFI Film Classics (London: British Film Institute, 1992); hereafter cited in text.

5.  The "almost final" script of 7 October 1938 specified more kinds of flowers: "[T]he grass is spangled with daisies, buttercups and red poppies .. . hollyhocks stand twenty feet in the air.... [T]he trees all have blossoms on them, suggesting a sort of permanent Spring—apple, cherry, peach and pear trees are everywhere, and a little stream runs near with huge lily-pads on it; the lilies are the size of barrel-tops." In this version the "exquisite fountain" has "water of all colors of the rainbow"—a "rainbow" theme reference that did not make it into the film (Harmetz, 55).

A further consideration for the art directors was that the Munchkins inhabiting this scene were to be played by midgets. According to Jack Martin, the sketch artist for the film, this helped determine the distinctive architecture of Munchkinland:

> Doors are only this high because the houses are for midgets. Windows are only this high. Flower boxes have to be low enough for midgets to water them. Then we put grass roofs on the houses and shaped them like mushrooms, and that was Munchkinland. (Harmetz, 212)

6. A scene actually filmed but omitted from the movie because of time constraints showed Dorothy and her friends returning to the Emerald City and parading through the streets in triumph after the destruction of the Witch; the missing scene (Appendix D) and a photograph of it are included in Langley.

7. The screenplay actually uses the word "goose-step" in describing the marching Winkies (Langley, 113), suggesting that the oblique references to Nazi Germany were intentional.

8. The Golden Cap was originally meant to play a part in the film, but as the Witch's personal "wishing cap" rather than the (morally neutral) means of controlling the Monkeys. The only direct reference to it was cut when the film underwent final editing; see Langley (83) for the complete passage.

9. In her final assessment of the film, Aljean Harmetz comments on the central importance of the Witch to children. "The most horrifying moment in the movie," she says, occurs when the face of Aunt Em in the crystal ball dissolves into that of the Witch, fusing the images of the nurturing mother and the angry mother into one.

> Small children meeting Margaret Hamilton hide behind their mothers' skirts and, if they can be coaxed out, scream at her that she was mean to take the dog. Other children become afraid. "Almost always they want me to laugh like the Witch," says Margaret Hamilton. "And sometimes when I go to schools, if we're in an auditorium, I'll do it. And there's always a funny reaction, like *Ye Gods, they wish they hadn't asked.*" (Harmetz, 296–97)

10. Ethan Mordden, "A Critic at Large: Judy Garland," *New Yorker,* 22 October 1990, 125.

11. Some critics have interpreted Dorothy's adventures in the film as a dream that reveals the psychological conflicts of the character. See, for example, Todd S. Gilman, " 'Aunt Em: Hate You! Hate Kansas! Taking the Dog. Dorothy': Conscious and Unconscious Desire in *The Wizard of Oz,*" *Children's Literature Association Quarterly* 20 (Winter 1995–1996): 161–67; hereafter cited in text.

12. Ursula K. Le Guin, "Why Are Americans Afraid of Dragons?" in *The Language of the Night: Essays on Fantasy and Science Fiction* (New York: G. P. Putnam's Sons, 1979), 40; hereafter cited in text.

# Selected Bibliography

## Primary Sources

*The Wizard of Oz.* [*The Wonderful Wizard of Oz,* 1900.] Critical Heritage Series, ed. Michael Patrick Hearn. New York: Schocken, 1983.

*The Life and Adventures of Santa Claus.* [1902] New York: Exposition Press, 1971.

*The Land of Oz.* [*The Marvelous Land of Oz.*] Chicago: Reilly and Britton, 1904.

*Ozma of Oz.* Chicago: Reilly and Britton, 1907.

*Dorothy and the Wizard of Oz.* Chicago: Reilly and Britton, 1908.

*The Road to Oz.* Chicago: Reilly and Britton, 1909.

*The Emerald City of Oz.* Chicago: Reilly and Britton, 1910.

*The Patchwork Girl of Oz.* Chicago: Reilly and Britton, 1913.

*Tik-Tok of Oz.* Chicago: Reilly and Britton, 1914.

*The Scarecrow of Oz.* Chicago: Reilly and Britton, 1915.

*Rinkitink in Oz.* Chicago: Reilly and Britton, 1916.

*The Lost Princess of Oz.* Chicago: Reilly and Britton, 1917.

*The Tin Woodman of Oz.* Chicago: Reilly and Britton, 1918.

*The Magic of Oz.* Chicago: Reilly and Lee, 1919.

*Glinda of Oz.* Chicago: Reilly and Britton, 1920.

## Secondary Sources
### Books and Parts of Books

Attebery, Brian. *The Fantasy Tradition in American Literature: From Irving to Le Guin.* Bloomington: Indiana University Press, 1980. Baum has a pivotal place in Attebery's history of American fantasy. The chapter on Baum offers a detailed critique of the Oz books and an analysis of Oz itself.

Baum, Frank Joslyn, and Russell P. MacFall. *To Please a Child: A Biography of L. Frank Baum, Royal Historian of Oz.* Chicago: Reilly and Lee, 1961. The first full-length biography—lacking documentation but enriched by the personal recollections of Baum's oldest son and including detailed descriptions of Baum's non-Oz writings and his dramatic ventures.

Bewley, Marius. "The Land of Oz: America's Great Good Place." In *Masks and Mirrors: Essays in Criticism,* 255–67. New York: Atheneum, 1970. Places the Oz books in the mainstream of American literature and discusses their resolution of "the dialectic between the pastoral vision and technology."

Carpenter, Angelica Shirley, and Jean Shirley. *L. Frank Baum: Royal Historian of Oz.* Minneapolis: Lerner Publications, 1992. An excellent biography for young people, carefully researched and abundantly illustrated.

Gardner, Martin, and Russel B. Nye. *The Wizard of Oz and Who He Was.* East Lansing, Mich.: Michigan State University Press, 1957. With a reprint of *The Wizard,* includes Gardner's short biography of Baum and Nye's analysis of the Oz books, their ethos and their humor.

Harmetz, Aljean. *The Making of "The Wizard of Oz": Movie Magic and Studio Power in the Prime of MGM—and the Miracle of Production #1060.* Introduction by Margaret Hamilton. New York: Alfred A. Knopf, 1977. The definitive account, based on personal interviews and primary sources, and well illustrated throughout.

Hearn, Michael Patrick. *The Annotated Wizard of Oz.* New York: Clarkson N. Potter, 1973. An invaluable source. Accompanying a complete text of *The Wizard,* with all the original illustrations, are numerous annotations on specific episodes, characters, allusions, and so forth. An appendix gives a detailed account of Baum's collaboration with Denslow.

———, ed. *The Wizard of Oz,* by L. Frank Baum. Critical Heritage Series. New York: Schocken, 1983. Along with a complete text of *The Wizard,* Hearn provides an excellent selection of appreciative and scholarly essays on the Oz books, beginning with Baum's own "Modern Fairy Tales."

Langley, Noel, Florence Ryerson, and Edgar Allan Woolf. *The Wizard of Oz: The Screenplay.* Edited by Michael Patrick Hearn. New York: Dell, 1989. The complete screenplay of the MGM movie, including (in appendices) scenes that were cut from the final version of the film. Hearn's introduction describes its complex evolution in painstaking detail.

Nathanson, Paul. *Over the Rainbow: "The Wizard of Oz" as a Secular Myth of America.* New York: State University of New York, 1991. An analysis of the book and the film from three perspectives: Jungian, Christian, and as "secular myth" expressing cultural tensions in American society.

Rushdie, Salman. *The Wizard of Oz*. BFI Film Classics. London: British Film Institute, 1992. A stimulating essay on the MGM film, focusing particularly on its theme of "home"; the accompanying short story, "On the Auction of the Ruby Slippers," takes a sharp look at America's ruby slipper fetish.

Snow, Jack. *Who's Who in Oz*. Chicago: Reilly and Lee, 1954. Snow's alphabetical compilation of 630 characters from the Oz books (by Baum and his successors), with pictures, makes an enjoyable reference work for young people.

Zipes, Jack. *Fairy Tales and the Art of Subversion: The Classical Genre for Children and the Process of Civilization*. 1983. Reprint, New York: Methuen, 1988. Places Baum and his utopia in a tradition of "subversive" nineteenth-century fantasy.

## Journal Articles

*The Baum Bugle: A Journal of Oz*. The quarterly journal of the International Wizard of Oz Club includes semischolarly, generously illustrated articles on a wide variety of topics related to Baum and his works, including movies and plays based on the Oz books.

Chaston, Joel D. "If I Ever Go Looking for My Heart's Desire: 'Home' in Baum's 'Oz' Books. *The Lion and the Unicorn* 18 (December 1994): 209–19. Contrasts the film's fixation on "home" with the less conventional attitudes toward home and family found throughout the Oz books.

Erisman, Fred. "L. Frank Baum and the Progressive Dilemma." *American Quarterly* 20 (Fall 1968): 616–23. Explores Baum's affinity with the Progressives, suggesting that the Oz books may have represented his solution to the Progressive dilemma.

Gilman, Todd S. " 'Aunt Em: Hate You! Hate Kansas! Taking the Dog. Dorothy': Conscious and Unconscious Desire in *The Wizard of Oz*." *Children's Literature Association Quarterly* 20 (Winter 1995–1996): 161–67. An ingenious Freudian interpretation of Dorothy's dream (in the MGM film) as an expression of her subconscious desires.

Hollister, C. Warren. "Oz and the Fifth Criterion." *Baum Bugle* (Winter 1971): 5–8. Also in Hearn 1983. Analyzes children's response to the Oz books, suggesting that the "three-dimensionality" of Oz itself is the source of their appeal.

Kopp, Sheldon. "The Wizard of Oz behind the Couch." *Psychology Today* 3 (March 1970): 70. Suggesting that *The Wizard* reveals Baum's dissatisfaction with Victorian ideas of character building, Kopp offers an amusing interpretation of the Wizard as wise therapist who helps others solve their own problems.

Littlefield, Henry M. "The Wizard of Oz: Parable on Populism." *American Quarterly* 16 (Spring 1964): 47–58. Also in Hearn 1983. Writing tongue-in-cheek, Littlefield interprets the characters of *The Wizard* as figures in a Populist allegory.

Sackett, S. J. "The Utopia of Oz." *Georgia Review* 14 (Fall 1960): 275–91. Also in Hearn 1983. A detailed and thoughtful analysis of the value system of Baum's democratic utopia.

Vidal, Gore. "On Rereading the Oz Books." *New York Review of Books,* 13 October 1977, 38–42. Also in Hearn 1983. One of the best appreciative essays on Baum, in which Vidal compares his responses as child and as adult reader of the Oz books.

# Index

# Index

# Index

# Index

# The Author

Suzanne Rahn is an associate professor in the English department at Pacific Lutheran University and director of the department's Children's Literature program. She is the author of *Children's Literature: An Annotated Bibliography of the History and Criticism* (Garland, 1980) and *Rediscoveries in Children's Literature* (Garland, 1995), as well as numerous articles on children's literature. She is also an associate editor of *The Lion and the Unicorn,* for which she has edited special issues on Heroes in Children's Literature, Historical Fiction and Nonfiction, and Nature and Ecology in Children's Literature. She earned a B.A. in literature from Scripps College in California and her Ph.D. from the University of Washington.

## The Editor

Robert Lecker is professor of English at McGill University in Montreal. He received his Ph.D. from York University. Professor Lecker is the author of numerous critical studies, including *On the Line* (1982), *Robert Kroetch* (1986), *An Other I* (1988), and *Making It Real: The Canonization of English-Canadian Literature* (1995). He is the editor of the critical journal *Essays on Canadian Writing* and of many collections of critical essays, most recent of which is *Canadian Canons: Essays in Literary Value* (1991). He is the founding and current general editor of Twayne's Masterwork Studies, and the editor of the Twayne World Authors Series on Canadian writers. He is also the general editor of G. K. Hall's Critical Essays on World Literature series.